Jane Tapsubei Creider grew up near Lake Nyanza (formerly Lake Victoria) in Kenya and after working in Kisumu and Nairobi she went to live in Canada. She now works as an artist in clay sculpture in London, Ontario; she is married with two children. Her articles on the language and culture of her people, the Nandi, have appeared in the *Journal of African Languages and Linguistics* and in *Anthropos*. She has written an introduction to the culture of the Nandi and, with her husband, a dictionary of the Nandi language; future writing plans include 'a novel dealing with the mentally handicapped and some stories for children in my own language'.

JANE TAPSUBEI CREIDER

Two Lives:
My Spirit and I

The Women's Press

First published by The Women's Press Limited 1986
A member of the Namara Group
34 Great Sutton Street, London EC1V 0DX

British Library Cataloguing in Publication Data
Creider, Jane Tapsubei
  Two lives: my spirit and I.
  1. Creider, Jane Tapsubei   2. Kenya, Biography
  I. Title
  967.6'204'0924   CT228.C/
  ISBN 0-7043-4006-2

Typeset by AKM Associates (UK) Ltd
Ajmal House, Hayes Road, Southall, London
Printed and bound in Great Britain by
Hazell Watson & Viney Ltd.,
Member of the BPCC Group,
Aylesbury, Bucks

Contents

Acknowledgments

I don't think that my trip to Canada would have been as good as it was if I hadn't met many wonderful people when I arrived. I was given a great deal of help and had much kindness shown to me. I would like to thank all the members of the Anthropology Department of the University of Western Ontario, and I would especially like to thank Dr Jim Freedman and his wife Alina who stood by my side with friendship and help when I first arrived. They took me in as though I was a member of their family. I would also like to thank Anne Donovan and Gary Graham, our son's godparents, and Dr Margaret Seguin who helped so enthusiastically to get our son baptized and christened.

The teachers of English as a Second Language at Fanshawe College helped me above and beyond the call of duty, and I will be grateful to them forever. My thanks go to Jeanne Lovelock, Chris Nath, Sandra McIntyre, Marjorie Reid, and the late Mrs Holroyd.

Many individuals with the name John have meant a great deal to me. I am almost superstitious about the name now. If someone is named John, I automatically assume that he will mean something special for me. My family doctor is John, my son's pediatrician is John, and I respect them both a great deal. I would also like to thank Dr John Tasker, who has lifted me up and given me new encouragement time and time again.

I would like to thank John Hammond and Jennifer Trønnes who spent many hours reading my manuscript and discussing it with me and likewise my husband for typing it and struggling with my Nandi syntax. Also Dr Mike Hall and his late wife Dr Bea Hall for encouragement and enthusiasm. Finally Dr Rhonda Cobham for her faith in the book. If there is anyone I have missed, I love them as well as those I have mentioned, and I thank them in my heart.

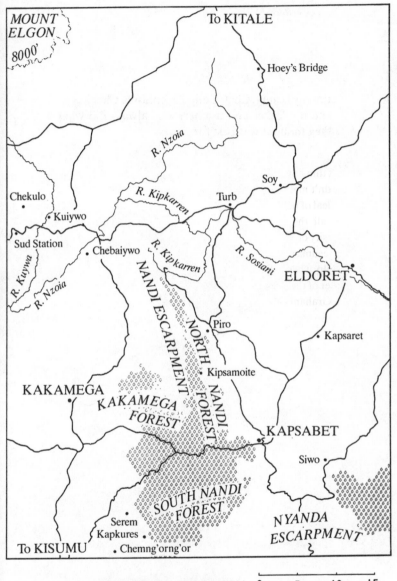

MOUNT ELGON

8000'

To KITALE

Hoey's Bridge

R. Nzoia

R. Kipkarren

Turb

Soy

Chekulo

Kuiywo

Sud Station

R. Kuywa

R. Nzoia

Chebaiywo

R. Kipkarren

R. Sosiani

ELDORET

Piro

Kapsaret

NANDI ESCARPMENT

Kipsamoite

NORTH NANDI FOREST

KAKAMEGA

KAKAMEGA FOREST

KAPSABET

Siwo

SOUTH NANDI FOREST

NYANDA ESCARPMENT

Serem

Kapkures

To KISUMU

Chemng'orng'or

35° EAST OF GREENWICH   0   5   10   15

Statute Miles

For my family, Chet, Colin Kigen, Julia Chepkogei, and my father and mother, who always did what they thought was best for me.

Introduction

I come from a people in East Africa called the Nandi and our people believe very strongly in spirits. The spirits are our ancestors. They are real people who are simply dead in this world but alive in the spirit world. We believe that when people die they join other ancestors who are dead. We have an expression that we use when someone is doing something which is dangerous. We say, 'Are the spirits calling you?'

These spirits have their own world. They are short, about two or three feet high, and are invisible to the living. Their world is below the surface of the earth, but they seem always to be close to water, and there are many people who have been rescued from drowning by spirits. When I was growing up, a family moved into the neighbourhood from a town about 30 miles away called Litein. The family had lived all their life near a large river called the Chemosit. The man of the house, James, had had a twin brother and as children the two boys used to play on a mudslide emptying into the river. One of the boys would slide down the hill, and the other would station himself part way down to catch him. One day, the older brother went down the slide so fast that James missed him. He twisted to try to catch him and flipped himself into the river. He lost consciousness, and when he came to, he was about five miles away and was being lifted out of the river by a man wearing a monkey-fur cape with a snuff-box on a chain round his neck and bracelets of iron round his arms. He didn't say much to the boy, just 'Don't look for your brother and don't play near the water again. Go home.' The body of his brother was never found. The man who had saved James was believed to have been a spirit, and he had saved James because it was not yet his time to go and nobody wanted him in the spirit world.

Another time, a man in our neighbourhood called Grandfather

Katele was caught in a whirlpool in the Kipkarren river. Everyone ran to try to help him with ropes and poles. He went down and bobbed up three times, then went down and didn't come up again. People kept looking for him for hours afterwards and finally gave up. The next day, he was at home. He said that he had heard ceremonial songs being sung and seen people round him, but that when he went to join them, they disappeared. When he got up, he discovered he was on the shore of the river and was soaking wet. When he came home in the morning, we children ran away from him because we thought he was dead.

The spirits stay with your family wherever you move. In a sense we share different aspects of one world with the spirits. We each have a time for our living. Our time is the day, and the spirits' time is the night. We sing lullabies to our children only during the day between ten and three, and the spirits sing to them at night. Sometimes, if you wake up at night, you can hear the spirits singing. Their life is a copy of ours. They keep cattle, raise children and in general have their own lives. Just as they are spirits to us, we are spirits to them.

During life, each person has a counterpart in the spirit world (and vice versa of course), but when you die you go to the spirit world as a new spirit, and you stay there and eventually become the counterpart to a new baby in this world. In fact you may choose to come back as more than one new baby, for one spirit may have a number of reincarnations. Back in the non-spirit world, people are never able to see their own spirit, because the spirit is them – it is not outside them to be seen. Nor can your spirit see you, because it is you, although other spirits can see you. We are not invisible to them.

There are some children who are very sensitive, and when you criticise them, they may have a terrible tantrum and become ill. We believe that it is really the spirit that is responsible for the way the child is behaving. In that case we must talk to the child to relax the spirit that is in its body and beg the spirit not to be angry over such little things. We talk to the spirit and say, 'We didn't mean anything bad. What's the matter with you? Can't you take a little criticism?'

Sometimes a spirit gets angry with a family. A child may suddenly fall ill for no apparent reason, and if she doesn't get better, it may be a malevolent spirit which is the cause of the sickness. The spirit must then be identified. This is done by putting four little twigs of wood in a tray of water and saying the names of possible spirits who could be responsible. When you give the name of a spirit which is causing the problem, all of the twigs will stand up in the water. When you know the spirit's name, you may start talking to it. 'Spirit of our clan, what is the matter? Why are you bothering that child? What has s/he done wrong to you? Leave the child alone. Let her be happy. If you want to come, you can come. Nobody will refuse your coming.' Then you pick up a twig and toss it to one side of the house saying, 'The good spirit who wants to stay with us, go sleep with the children on the east side.' Then you take another twig and toss it to another side of the house inviting the good spirits to stay with the lambs and goat kids. Next you take a twig and toss it to the west side of the house inviting the spirits to be with the men and where the milk is stored. Finally you take a twig and toss it out of the house, saying, 'If you are going to be a bad spirit, then get out of the house.'

If you visit me and are of the same clan as me, and I give you food, you must share it with the spirits. You take bites of food and spit them out to the spirits in various directions. When you travel, your spirits travel with you.

Among the Nandi, spirits are always associated with the husband's side of a family. Let me try to explain this. When a woman marries she becomes the controller of the things in the household she and her husband set up together – the house, the livestock and the land. These things are initially provided by the husband's family, and the wife and husband will care for them and pass them on to their children. A woman usually thinks that the things are hers to pass on to her children because her husband may marry another wife and set up a second household. So a woman is responsible for what she will give to her own children. Both husband and wife have equal rights to what they own, but neither can dispose of any of it without the consent of the other. A woman receives nothing from her own home, because her brothers will marry other women who will receive everything in the household she grew up in. Similarly the spirits associated with the husband's line are passed on by the mother to her children. The spirits residing in her childhood home will become the children of her brothers and their wives. So you could say that spirits are inherited in the same way as other things. A woman can't pass on the spirits of her father's household because they will be going to the children of her brothers.

The Nandi believe very strongly in spirit reincarnation. With us, however, no one is ever able to see back to their own spirit the way some people in Western society believe they do. Parents or relatives who knew a spirit in a former existence will recognise that spirit in a new incarnation and can recall the events of that spirit's life. Many children are born resembling their past spirit exactly. My Grandmother Gogo had been blind in her left eye since childhood. When she was reborn as a baby boy, Malakwen, the boy's left eye was closed. This was the way Gogo's spirit let the grown-ups know who had been reborn. One of my uncles went to fight in World War II, was shot in the hip and returned home to die of the wound. When he was born as my brother Moses, he had a hole in his hip. My grandmother immediately told us not to be scared, and as soon as Moses was named, the hole disappeared. The spirit of my sister Chemonos liked to smoke a pipe. When my mother was pregnant, she wanted to smoke very much even though she had never smoked before. After Chemonos was born, my mother no longer wanted to smoke, but the baby smacked her lips exactly the way someone does when she is smoking a pipe.

A woman can discover who the spirit of her child is during her pregnancy. A spirit may come and identify himself or herself to the mother in a dream and that way the woman can know who her baby is.

It is very hard to explain how spirit reincarnation works, especially to a people who don't practise it and for whom it is not part of the culture. I believe myself that the spirit is a real thing even though you can't see back yourself to your own spirit. I think that even people who don't believe in the method of spirit reincarnation still get their spirits from past relatives.

I didn't think that spirit reincarnation was real until Grandmother Gogo was reborn as my brother Malakwen. Since I was around, I knew immediately that the baby might be my grandmother because his left eye was closed. However, I was just guessing. I had been taught that when a baby was born you had to look for signs of its past spirit. After that it is necessary to hold a ceremony to see if the baby agrees with the spirit name you give to it. If the baby does agree with its name, then it will sneeze, urinate or hiccup to show you. If the name is not right, then the baby won't do any of these things. In the case of my grandmother, my guess was right. When the baby was given the name Gogo, he sneezed and urinated. My grandmother had come back as a man. She didn't like being a woman in my father's dynasty any more.

As I watched Malakwen grow in his present life, it amazed me how identical he was to his past spirit. He had a very gentle voice, and he didn't get excited no matter what you told him, just like his grandmother. The thing that made me most believe that the spirit was real was that when I talked to young grandmother who I know as my brother in his present life, he always answered me the way old grandmother had in her life. There is one example that I can still remember.

One day my sisters and I were sitting on the hill in front of our house and young grandmother was there too. All of a sudden, one of my sisters grabbed my sunglasses. I spoke to my sister in anger and took my sunglasses back.

'If you were my child, I would strangle you!' I said.

When my sister left, young grandmother called my name.

'Tapsubei, you know your sister was just wanting to try on your glasses because she loves you. I don't think she meant anything bad,' he said to me.

Young grandmother was not more than four years old at that time. The words he used were the same words my grandmother had used six years before in her past life when I was fighting with the same sister over a blanket.

This is not the only way he showed how much like his spirit he was. For one thing, he had a way of casting aspersions with his eyes when you said something he didn't like or didn't believe. His past spirit had done exactly the same thing. When you told her something she didn't believe, she wouldn't disagree to your face, but would wait until you turned away and then make a face about you to someone else. This is not something men in our culture do, but Malakwen couldn't help himself because of who he was.

We believe that a spirit can see you, but that you can't see it. Since we can't see the spirits, no one finds death easy even though they know that they will return as a spirit.

We also don't believe in punishment after death. We think that if you do something bad, you will be punished right here on earth. We don't believe in a heaven either. We just believe that all spirits go down to live with other spirits. They live just like us. They also don't have any heaven or hell, but live by the same customs we live by.

When I was a little girl I loved very much to listen to Grandmother

5

Gogo tell me about my spirit past. I was very close to my grandmother. She and I would often go off and sit alone together after I had finished doing some work for her. She would thank me for the good job I had done and call me by a name of praise such as 'Cheptap Ng'erech – or Eng Abay' or 'Cheptap Kiptech-kong' Eng' Lomet'. These names were a source of mystery to me at first; it is very difficult to translate them into English. The first name means something like 'daughter of one who is surrounded by happiness', and the second means 'daughter of Mr Eyes-which-show-humility-and-respect'. The first expression literally means 'the road smiles with Abay', and 'Abay' means to go to a house when you have a child which has recently been born to ask for some milk and a name of praise for the new-born child. If many people go to your house in this way you are greatly respected. This respect would be accorded you because you were a great hero and had gone on many successful cattle-raiding expeditions.

Another name my grandmother called me was 'Tapsub Terikin Kòrari'. These three words mean 'woman who grabbed a Terik (a member of a tribe from whom the Nandi raided cattle) and shocked the man so that instead of fighting back he laughed and gave up'. The names she called me led me to believe that I had been someone else in the past and that that someone had also been a woman. When I first heard this I was astonished. I tried to feel the past. I would lie down and try to imagine what I was like then, but I couldn't see anything.

One day I asked my grandmother, 'Do you think someday I will see all those things you are telling me about?'

'Yes,' she said, 'when you grow a little older you will visit your son and your brother. You've even seen one of the people from your spirit past already.'

'Who?' I said.

'You.'

I was even more confused. I was too young for my grandmother to explain how the entire culture worked to me. I gradually learned that the Nandi named their children after their ancestors. They believed that the name they gave to a child was really a name of one of their ancestors who had come back. They would always tell a child who she was, how many children she had had, and what her husband had been like.

The Nandi also believe that spirit is more important than genes. A natural born and an adopted child both have spirits waiting for them when they arrive. Nandi believe that genes are important for causing life to be in the first place, but, like a seed, genes can be planted anywhere in the world. For example, a man can go to China or any other far-away place, meet a woman for a night, and just like that the genes will remain there. A spirit, however, stays in the family line for ever. One may wonder why genes can go out of the family when spirit can't, when we believe that both spirit and genes come from the husband's side. Well, there is more to it than this, but just because a man has a spirit inside to pass on doesn't mean he can pass it out wherever he chooses. He has to have a woman who has gone through a ritual with him and been given a blessing by the family with him for the spirit ancestors of his family to be reincarnated in his children. That is why a spirit never goes out of the family. I could go on endlessly talking about Nandi customs because everything one does is connected with them.

The first family tree is a picture of my past.

A Western reader may well be confused because there is no way in other cultures that someone could be my father and my second cousin at the same time. The family tree is a picture of the way we Nandi see things. To make things easier, there is a second tree which looks at my family from a Western point of view, as a reader unfamiliar with spirit reincarnation might think of it.

I am the third Tapsubei to be reincarnated. The first went to Tapsubei's brother, the second went to her son, and the third went to her cousin. The one who went to her cousin is now the writer of this book. If the other two were to write their stories, the stories would be the same, except there might be more detail. The reason for that is that the first two times Tapsubei was reincarnated in the family she lived in the past. I owe the little I know about my spirit ancestor to Grandmother Gogo.

7

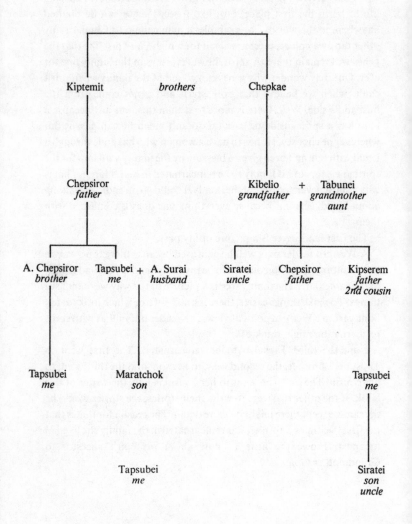

A portion of my family tree as we Nandi see it

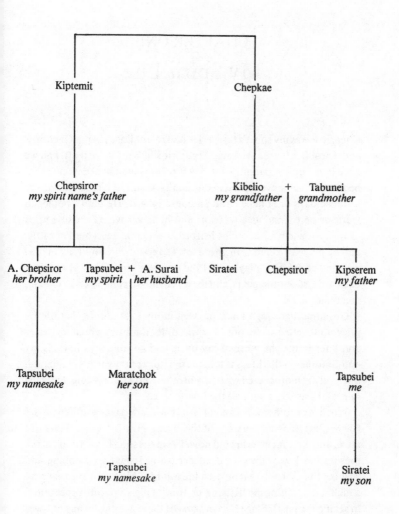

The same tree as Westerners see it

CHAPTER ONE

My Spirit Life

Chepsiror was my spirit's father. He had two children, Arap Chepsiror and Tapsubei. Tapsubei is me. My spirit's father was well off, and we were loved by our parents a lot. My brother was spoiled beyond belief because he knew everything in our family would be his. In our culture in those days only male children could inherit. He didn't bother to learn or be trained as a warrior, and he never went on cattle raids against the enemy. Instead he learned how to manage a herd of cattle, and he played around with girls a lot. I suppose you could say that he was one of the first 'playboys of the non-western world'. My parents had cattle, sheep and goats, and these provided a complete diet of milk, meat and blood.

Grandmother Gogo knew me well in my past life. In that life we grew up together as friends. She was older than I by about six years, and later in life she married my uncle and became my aunt. As my grandmother in this life, she told me the story of my spirit's childhood. She said my mother died when my brother and I were young. I was the one who was stuck with all the housework.

When my brother was 15 and I was 16 we had to face another crisis. I (the writer) was told the story of this by my spirit's brother. He is still alive, and is about 80 years old now. From the time I was a child in my present life I was always full of curiosity. I went on thinking and wishing that I knew what my past life was like. My father even gave me a nickname, calling me 'Kibung'ut' (one of a group which specialised in seeing the past). Since I wasn't one of these people, he meant I was sticking my nose into the past. The first thing I did when I met my ancestor's brother was to be as close to him as I could. Then, little by little, I would ask him, 'Brother?'

'Yes?' he would say.

'Was I close to you?'

'Yes, sister, you were the only mother I ever knew after our mother died. Our father was a lonely man after our mother died, so he became ill when you were 16 and I was 15. He was so sick that he began to lose hope. He decided to let us know that he might die any day. He didn't tell us in many words. He just called us, "My children, come and sit and listen. I want to let you know what I have been thinking."

'He told me that I was a big man now, and that I should be initiated and get married as soon as I came out of initiation. "Then you and your wife will look after your sister Tapsubei," he said. Then he went on speaking. "I feel like the world won't be mine for very long." '

So my brother was initiated right away and then was given a wife. The next was me.

After I was initiated people came right away to ask for me for their sons to marry. The process is a little like a Miss World contest in reverse. First there are the contestants, the male suitors (or rather their parents). Then there are the judges. These are all relatives of the girl. Usually the relatives do most of the judging and the immediate family goes along with their decisions. In my case, however, my father joined in the deliberations because he had someone definite in mind. He wanted to marry me to an old man whom he had decided to honour because he was kind-hearted. The old man was so poor that no one would give their daughter to him in marriage for fear he wouldn't be able to provide for her. He also didn't have anything to pay the bride's family. Our custom is for the groom and his family to give some cattle and other livestock to the bride's family in exchange for their daughter. This old man could only afford a very small down-payment, and it was understood that he would probably never be able to pay the rest.

I was not present when the groom and his runner-up were being chosen. It is the custom that the prospective bride stays in a different room, and the judges speak so quietly that she can't hear a single word. When they have finished their deliberations they call her and say, 'We like so-and-so and so-and-so. What do you think of them?'

That means they are giving her a choice. If, however, they don't want to give her any choice, they will say, 'We like so-and-so, and we think that so-and-so (someone else) is the runner-up. Do you have any questions?' This gives her a chance to voice her objections if she has any. If she thinks he is worthless, or if he chases after women, or if he is a 'Kipyat-ko' (someone who tries to sneak into women's houses under the cover of darkness), she says so.

The judges will determine which of these objections are serious enough to warrant correction, and then they tell the suitor, 'We accept you to marry our daughter, but there are a few changes that the girl wants you to make before you marry her. Do you think you can agree to do this?' The suitor will say yes because he wants to get married right away, and the judges will tell him what the required changes are. The girl then hands out oil for her parents to anoint the groom's parents with. That signals that everything is all right, and that the girl has agreed to marry the boy.

This is the way everything is done if the girl and the boy know each other well because they are same age and have dated one another. But in my case the situation was completely different because I would never have dreamt in a million years that I would have anything to do with that old man. I thought that everything was wrong with him. He was thin, tall and always wore the ragged clothes of a hunter. He carried a shoulder-bag with a little meat with him wherever he went. If he cooked and had leftovers, he would put them in his bag the next day. But the rags and the bag weren't what bothered me. What if he should go blind of old age a few years after marrying me? Who would go hunting for food? And who would carry the bag with the meat around for him? He wasn't even a Nandi; he came from a tribe called the Akie. So I told my father and his relatives that everything about the old man was wrong and, what was worse, nothing could be changed. He couldn't make himself any younger, he could never learn to become a warrior and a raider of cattle, and he would always remain poor.

'What has gone wrong with my father?' I asked. 'Is the old man even going to live until I come out of initiation (which could be a year's time) to marry me?'

Other important questions were what I would eat and what I would wear after he married me. Curiously, his name itself was not very encouraging, for he was called Mr Surai which means 'Mr Shabby'. I told my father that if he thought I was going to worry endlessly about what to eat and what to wear after getting married, he was very mistaken.

In spite of everything I said, I lost the fight. My father answered my questions in a split second. He told me that marrying an old man was not something to be ashamed of.

'He is not something you are going to wear on your face or something you are going to compare with other women saying, "Look, mine is older" or "Mine is younger".'

He pointed out that if I had children, they wouldn't be old. He also told me that the old man wouldn't have to hunt again, and that I wouldn't have to worry about anything at all because he was going to give me cattle, goats and sheep.

This answered my objections, and so I had to marry the old man, but it was still unsatisfactory. Our tribe's custom was not to allow wealth to go outside the male line permanently. So both my father and I knew that the livestock was only a loan, and that after I had passed away, the cattle and smaller stock would go back to my brother or to his sons, and nothing would remain for my own sons.

In those days a man and a woman had completely different fields. A woman's job was to be the mother of the children, and to make the home warm and happy for a man to come into. She didn't have to worry about anything outside the house; that was all men's work. Life like that was just as smooth as silk. A family could easily spend a year without an argument because everybody knew their own line of work.

Things were slightly different if you married an older man. For example, he would help you with the housework if you got behind with it. An old man would take more responsibility for you and he would listen to you more than a young man would. This was because his own mother wouldn't be around to provide support for you as a newly-wed. So he was both a husband and a mother-in-law.

The mother-in-law is very important in Nandi society. If a family has a number of sons who marry, all their wives will be trained by the mother. The last wife and her husband will remain with the in-laws because, according to our custom, the last-born son is the one who looks after the parents when they are old.

I've talked only about last-born sons because, in Nandi society, it is the sons who take care of their parents. But what if the last born is a girl? In that case the mother would always want to go to visit her daughter after she was married, but she would run into problems with her son-in-law. He would think that the mother-in-law was destroying the household by taking the power he has over his wife. The husband can ask his wife to do something quite unreasonable, and if she refuses he can become furious.

'Why didn't you do what I told you to do? What were you doing all day long? Did you wait until I left the house and then start "circling the fireplace" with your mother talking and talking all day? Why did you leave your mother and get married if you knew you still had a lot to talk about? If you ask my opinion I would say that your mother has completely destroyed your brain with all that talking.'

When many nasty words have been said, the poor mother-in-law will start getting the message. If she is clever she will leave before the matter gets bad publicity in the neighbourhood. The custom is not to interfere with your daughter's life when she is married. The reason is to avoid the kind of argument I've just described.

The reason the mother-in-law trains the daughter-in-law is to avoid a similar mess. If you don't learn what kinds of things your husband likes you'll run into trouble. To avoid this you get lessons from your husband's own mother. Then if someday you cook something for your husband which he doesn't like and he asks you if this is the kind of food your mother cooks for your father, you can say, 'No, this is the kind of food your mother taught me to cook for you when I got married.'

Nandi men never want to know the truth about their mothers. Anything bad which you say is just like criticising the Statue of Liberty.

What I've talked about so far is what can happen if things really get out of hand. In fact, in our society, a mother-in-law and a son-in-law are supposed to show each other a great deal of respect. If the mother-in-law should visit, the two do not shake hands but greet each other from a distance. When the mother-in-law is inside, the son-in-law usually sits outside. If he really has to go in, he stays a good distance away from his wife's mother. If they talk to each other, they only say a few polite sentences.

The Nandi believe that you shouldn't stay around someone you have to respect too long, because everyone has their own faults and their own way of life. There are other people whom one must respect (and avoid), but in-laws especially are the people a man doesn't want to have trouble with. Such trouble might give him and his family a bad record and make it difficult for him to get a second wife or for his younger brothers to marry.

In my spirit life I was tall, beautiful, slender, long-limbed and brown-skinned, with a well-shaped head, fine features, an attractive smile, kinky black hair, and a stubborn character indeed.

About eighty years ago, Nandi customs were still followed rigidly and were not scattered from sunrise to sunset the way they are now. It didn't matter how powerful you were or how stubborn you were, you had to follow the traditional rules. So I tried to be a good wife to my husband. We lived well, ate well, and we agreed on almost everything. After a while I learned not to be bothered by his age. My husband learned to look after cattle and to live like a Nandi. He was even better than a Nandi because he used to help me with all kinds of work. Perhaps men and women helped each other in this way in the country he had come from.

Eventually we had a son, Marat Chok. The wealth of my family continued to expand. Father had given me three goats when I got married and now there were six. It was the same with the sheep and the cattle. By that time, however, my father had passed away, and my brother made it very clear that it was his wealth and that I could not just do what I wanted with it. For example, I couldn't slaughter a goat or a cow for visiting friends without asking him. Sometimes I would get no for an answer, which had never happened when my father was alive.

I began to realise that I had started out with nothing and was going to end up with nothing. It made me even sadder to think that my son might have the same problems. I decided I would have to do something about it. One evening I asked my husband, 'What should we do? You know we have a son now, and he must have things to begin his life with.'

My husband told me that his people lived from day to day by hunting. They didn't plan for tomorrow or next week. Our son would be taught to live in the same way – I was not very happy to hear that.

In those days a woman lived only in the company of other women. You couldn't go and ask a man to help you raid cattle. Raiding was a dangerous business, many men lost their lives and no man would take a woman along. But raiding was the only thing I could do to have something of my own and to give my son a better future.

I had an idea of which people to raid from. Our custom didn't allow us to steal from our own and closely related tribes. One day I reached the decision to go raiding, by myself.

I headed into the trackless wilderness. There was no map, and I was guided only by the sun. I knew I was to go west. I would follow the sunset until I reached a place called Chemng'orng'or, the border between Nandi and another group of tribes called the Luyia. I didn't take anything with me except for some small gourds in which I carried a little milk. But it didn't matter really, for I had good looks, good manners and good health. I must have been very young, maybe about twenty, and attractive, because everywhere I went, people tried to make me stay with them. I would stay a couple of days, or until I found out how to get further towards my destination, and then I would disappear.

I travelled like that across the wilderness until I reached a place called Kapkeben. The people there spoke like the Nandi, but with a very strong accent so that sometimes a Nandi had trouble understanding them. I found a man gardening, and asked him if he knew of a place called Chemng'orng'or.

'Yes, I do,' he said, and I asked him how far it was. He told me that it was about a mile and a half, and he asked me if I knew anyone there.

'No,' I said. 'I just want to see it. I've heard that there are some big caves there.'

He knew that I didn't belong to his tribe, the Terik, so he asked me if I had some relatives to stay with. I said that I didn't but that I was sure I would find some place to stay for a few days until I had seen the caves, and then I would go back. He asked me to stay with him.

The country was very dry and full of rocks. It was so poor that people always wanted to leave to go to Mosop which is where I came from. This made me feel that the family I was staying with were not enemies so I asked them if they knew where someone could go to raid. They said yes, so I made a deal with Terigin, one of the sons of the family. I told him that if he helped me to go raiding and if we succeeded, I would take him back with me to Mosop so that he could start a new life in that rich land. He agreed right away.

We started immediately to plan our route and our course of action. I was given a sword and spear, a warrior's traditional equipment, and we set off. We travelled until we reached Chemng'orng'or, and the first thing we saw was a lot of sheep. The shepherd taking care of them was sleeping. I called Terigiń and told him, 'This is it. We won't go any further, we'll just take these animals.'

'Oh no,' he said. 'We haven't reached the place we are going to yet. These sheep belong to Terik. They are people just like me, and I speak the same language they do.'

'You're not doing this for yourself,' I said. 'You're doing it for me. You take care of the sheep, and I'll look after the shepherd.'

He didn't disagree any more, but pulled out his sword, and started taking the sheep. The shepherd was still asleep when we left. When we had gone about two miles we heard the sound of someone running after us. I told my friend to go ahead with the sheep and that I would deal with the shepherd. I pulled aside and waited behind a bush. When he came alongside me I grabbed him around his shoulders. He looked at me and started laughing, out of fear.

'Don't be afraid,' I told him. 'Tell me what you are running for.'

'I'm running after my sheep,' he said. 'Did you see them?'

'Yes,' I said, 'I met a lot of men carrying weapons and taking sheep, and I'm sure some of them are still around. If I were you I wouldn't move from here.'

I left the shepherd staring after me, open mouthed. Then I went after the sheep. When Terigin saw me he asked, 'How did you get away from him?' He thought I must have killed the shepherd because I had a sword.

'I didn't kill him,' I told my friend, 'if that's what you're thinking.'

'What happened?' he asked. 'Did he get away from you?'

'No,' I said. 'I left him with the understanding that he wasn't to follow us.'

My friend was afraid that the shepherd would get more men to come after us. I decided to go on in a different direction, hoping that he would be less afraid, but it didn't seem to help. Terigin wanted us to go in the direction of Mosop. But I wanted to plunge to the south-east into a great unknown forest called Kaimosi. I knew the forest was very dangerous, and we would be less likely to be followed there. People used to believe the forest was inhabited by animals called *kerinik* ('Nandi bears') that could grab people and eat their brains out, and by monsters called *chemosinik* who were people by day and animals by night that could swallow a person whole. I just planned to pray to my ancestors telling them, '*Omuta mutyo leye koinya ondowa*'. 'Take me slowly, people of my family. Go ahead of me and scare away everything that wants to hurt me'.

But Terigin didn't want to trust to luck any more, and he became really angry at me.

'I have no feeling of gratitude from you at all,' he said. 'I think you are stubborn and I have decided that you have the wrong personality for me. I had better let you go your way, and I go mine.'

Between you and me I think he was afraid of the monsters in the forest. I told him that was all right with me, and I gave him directions to my home. There were no roads in those days and one gave directions by telling the person what country he would pass through on his way to where he was going.

I parted with him in mid-afternoon at a place called Siginwai. He went back to his home, and I headed towards the forest. I had decided to sleep at a place called Chebaraa and to go through the forest in the morning. I was hoping that the monster-animals would have gone to sleep for the day.

Meanwhile, people at home were asking everybody they met if they had seen me. Some people would say, 'we saw her heading that way.' My relatives went on asking until they worked out that I had gone to Chemng'orng'or and eventually they reached Terigin's home.

He told them I had been there but that I had left after I'd got what I came for.

Now no one from home knew what I had come for and they learned from my friend that I had gone raiding. They were very surprised because they thought I had run away for some unknown reason or for one of the usual reasons like a drunken or nagging husband.

Terigin told them everything. Since he knew where I was heading, he asked my people if he could go with them to show them the road. They agreed, and they all set off after me.

Meanwhile, I marched through the forest with my sheep safely. My dream was starting to come true. At that point I was no longer afraid of the enemy coming after me or of animals eating me up. I was in Nandi land, and all I had to do was walk slowly and let the sheep graze. My relatives were behind me following the spoor of the sheep through the forest and when they realised that I had got through safely they were very relieved. They decided to hurry home to tell people not to worry, that Tapsubei was coming. The trip to Mosop from there would take a person travelling alone only about an hour, but sheep are impossible to hurry. They never walk straight but go in a group sticking their heads together and meandering all over the place. So the trip of one hour took me an entire afternoon, and I got home in the evening.

When I got there everybody was waiting to cheer for me. My son, husband, brother, his wife, other relatives, and Terigin were all waiting for me to celebrate. When the celebration was finished, life went back to normal. I went back to being a housewife and my husband went on looking after cattle and sheep. Terigin decided to seek a new life in Nandi country because that was what he had always wanted. Land in Nandi country was not owned privately in those days. People used just to move around wherever they wanted. For a non-native, however, it was not so simple. He could be killed by Nandi people thinking he was an enemy trying to raid cattle. Therefore we had to adopt Terigin. That was the only thing we could do so that he could live freely like anyone else, move around, raid with other men, marry a Nandi girl, and have a home.

Adoption was common in Nandi society. For example, when warriors went raiding they might stumble upon a person of the tribe whose cattle they had raided. Instead of killing this person, the warriors would just take him along with them. The warrior who actually took the person would be called 'Chelulei Mabarei'. This means someone who instead of killing an enemy captures him and adopts him to give him a new life.

Since the Nandi didn't have any prisoners or slaves, the only thing they could do when they captured somebody was to adopt him and give him freedom to live as an independent person. He would be adopted by a particular Nandi family and from them receive a name, membership in a clan and membership in a *pororiet* (a land-based political unit). The name was usually a very general one, such as 'Arap Gogo' (son of grandmother) or 'Arap Chorwa' (son of a friend). If it was felt to be appropriate, the adopting family was prepared to give him the name of one of its ancestors. This meant that the man was really part of the family line, and his children would belong to it.

But the adoptee could also choose to be one of his own ancestors. He might choose to do this out of loneliness in order to feel that he was still with his own people. In this case the man would not be part of the lineage of the adopting family, but would found his own lineage. The purpose of adult adoption in Nandi was not to acquire another body for the family line, but really to facilitate the foreigner's settling in Nandi and to give him a place to begin his new life from. In this respect it was very different from adopting a child. An adopted child became a full member of the family as a matter of course, and it didn't matter if he was picked up in the forest or on the street. After the child was given the name of an ancestor of the family, it was entitled to just the same respect by outsiders and insiders as anyone else in the family.

So we adopted Terigin. He married and settled in Nandi, had children, and today is a very old man.

My husband and I had only one son, and we lived very happily together. We raised our son well, and he grew up with good manners and even became something of a hero, a living legend in his time, because of his skill in raiding. His name is Marat Chok. That means someone who can't wear a sword because he is so thin that the belt of the sword sheath can't stay around his waist. It would just drop down if he wore it. He grew up to be a really great warrior. At the age of 14, when he was a young boy before initiation, he had already learned to use weapons and went raiding with other men. By the time he came out of initiation, World War II had started. The British during that time were still looking for more men to fight against the Italians in East Africa, so they took our son when he was just 17. He went to war leaving me in good health, but by the time he came back, I had already been sick and was near death. I was just waiting to see him again.

I died of food poisoning. I left my husband and Marat Chok. My husband at that time was really old, too. He couldn't be by himself, so my brother and his wife had to look after him. Eventually Marat Chok got married. After he had had a couple of children, I was reborn as Tapsubei, the author of this book. When I learned he was my son in an earlier life, I used to visit him. Even though I was a little girl, I was treated as his mother. His children were always happy to see me. They called me grandma although some of them were older than I was. Their mother liked to call me 'mother-in-law'. That was nice; I liked it very much, but what really made me happy was being there with my son. I thought he was the best-looking person that I had ever seen. Anything that he said seemed good to my way of thinking. I took my job as his mother very seriously, and I didn't want to hear anyone say anything bad about him. I would cry and ask the person who was speaking about him, 'Why are you saying bad things about my son? Why don't you like him?' I would be really angry. When I visited the family I would usually stay for three to four days, and that was very hard on them. So if they wanted to talk about us, instead of referring to us as Marat Chok and Tapsubei, they would invent names and talk about 'Kibet' and 'Chemutai' so as not to upset me.

Marat Chok and my present father are the same age, too. They spent a lot of time together when they were growing up. They raided together a great deal and had a lot of secret shared places for use when raiding. They are still good friends, and I think that they will probably never change, but will remain friends for ever. I didn't find all of this out when I was a little girl, however. When Marat Chok visited us I thought he was just visiting me because I was his mother. My sisters and my brother thought the same way too. I remember one day when my son visited us and I was out looking after cattle with my present sister, and the other children were at home when he arrived. They left right away to find me to tell me the news. They came running saying to one another, 'I'm going to tell her first.'

'What?' I asked them.

'You would never guess who came to visit today,' they said.

'Who?' I said. 'Tell me!'

'Your son!'.

We were all very happy and jumped up and down. Especially me – I was completely ecstatic.

CHAPTER TWO
A Nandi Girl of East Africa

In the latter part of the fifteenth century, the Nandi people migrated from Mt Elgon in Western Kenya to a point on the Nandi escarpment overlooking Lake Nyanza (Lake Victoria). From there they gradually grew and expanded to the north and east moving towards what are now the towns of Kitale and Eldoret. In the latter stages of this expansion, they encountered and defeated the Masai in numerous engagements. They were like the Masai in many ways: the keeping of cattle was the most important thing in the world to them, and they were very fierce and militaristic. The raiding of neighbouring peoples for cattle was the main occupation of the young men of the tribe. Like the Masai, the Nandi felt they were superior to all the other people they encountered, and this feeling of superiority applied also to the British. During the nineteenth century, the Nandi never allowed Arab slave-trading expeditions to pass through their country. When, towards the end of the nineteenth century, European expeditions began to pass near Nandi, and the Europeans tried to trade with the Nandi, their caravans were considered fair game for Nandi warriors, at least as far as the livestock travelling with the caravans was concerned.

Beginning in 1895, the British began to send military expeditions into Nandi in an attempt to intimidate and subjugate them in the way they had been able to with all the other tribes in East Africa. These expeditions met with little success, and did little to increase Nandi admiration for the British, since the armies were nearly entirely made up of Sudanese and Ugandan mercenaries. The Nandi didn't think much of a people who couldn't even fight their own battles! It was even more comical to the Nandi to watch the British being carried (!) by their soldiers on litters through Nandi land. Not only could they not fight, they couldn't even walk! It was also a case of overkill. In a typical engagment, hundreds of Sudanese soldiers were shooting at a handful of Nandi warriors.

In 1905, the British sent an expedition consisting of regular mercenary soldiers, Masai who had been forced into service for the occasion, and a great deal of artillery. After five months the Nandi were defeated. In addition to having their cattle, sheep and goats confiscated and their houses burned down, the Nandi lost control of over 1,250 square miles of land and were confined to a reserve of only 700 square miles. To add insult to the injury, the British gave the lost land to European settlers. In 1919 two further pieces of land were taken for settlers.

For a very long time, at least up until World War II, the Nandi had no interest in the British or in westernisation with the exception of a very small number of people who were affected by missionaries. Later on, boys were put into school not to learn new ways of life, but to learn English so that when the fighting with the British resumed they would understand what the enemy were saying. Girls weren't sent to school because they had nothing to do with fighting.

When I was little, one of the people I loved most was my father's mother, Grandmother Gogo. She was a typical Nandi traditionalist. She didn't change as the times changed, and she wanted us to be traditional like her. She told me all about the Nandi past and I loved listening to her stories. She was getting old, and there was a lot about modern society that she didn't understand and didn't like. She had only travelled by car once in her lifetime, and she had been ill. She told me that she couldn't sit up in the car, but had had to lie down flat and cover her head with her clothes. Every time she tried to sit up, the trees were running and her eyes felt like they were going to pop out of her head, and after she got to her destination her whole body was numb. She felt she had gone mad, and it took her three months to recover. The fact that so few roads in Kenya were paved then probably made her ride all the more terrifying.

Grandma spoke only two languages, Nandi and Masai. She also knew one word in Swahili, *kwenda*, which means 'go', but she thought it was a European word because she had heard it from the British when they were settling on farms in Africa. So I spent a lot of time trying to explain which languages were European and which were African.

Grandma didn't like modern soap with its perfume. She said that it made her smell like a foreigner so she always told whoever was going to get soap for her not to get the one with the smell. Another thing she couldn't stand at all was the radio. She called it a bumblebee. The only time anyone was allowed to listen to the radio was during the daytime. As soon as it was about five in the afternoon she would come and say, 'Shut off the bumblebee, the cattle are coming home.' Her idea was that the radio would upset the cattle completely, and that they might even run away in the middle of the night. She also thought that the radio was for poor people and that if we kept listening to it, we were asking for poorness. She didn't like a language other than Nandi being spoken in the family, and because the radio was in English she thought it was destroying the family's traditions. The radio also talked about what was going on outside our society, and that was of absolutely no use to Grandma Gogo; she said that we had no reason to know about such things. As far as she was concerned, the radio was turning us into devils instead of children. In more modern language you could say that she thought that the radio contributed to the delinquency of minors!

Grandmother didn't want children to grow up too quickly; she wanted us to learn things slowly as we grew. She said that there was no need to learn anything from the radio. Our parents were good enough.

Grandma lived a good life. She lived to be 95 or more. There were no members of her generation, or 'age-set', in the neighbourhood where we lived. The few who were still alive lived far away. Everyone else who was 'old' in our neighbourhood was younger than 60. Grandma belonged to the generation called *kaplelach che mi chego mo*, which means 'the age-set with milk (wealth) in abundance'. (Nandi people had seven cyclic age-sets. Each one lasted fifteen years, and when the last set had finished, the cycle started over again.) She had had seven co-wives in her marriage with my grandfather, but six of these had passed away long ago with my grandfather. Only one co-wife, the youngest, was left and Grandma was the next youngest. The two of them lived like friendly sisters in one place until their children were old enough to take care of them. Even after they separated, each to her own children, they still were very fond of each other. They shared their feelings about their children and helped each other in raising them. Since Grandma Gogo was older, her co-wife usually sought her advice when she had problems with her children. Grandma's voice was heeded by all the children. In our society when an older person spoke, the younger people were supposed to listen.

My grandpa was a wealthy man. When he died he left a lot of wealth with his wives and his children, so no one had any problems as far as that was concerned. But when the British came to Africa, everyone's wealth was endangered. Pastoralists like the people of my tribe, whose wealth was only in cattle, suffered the biggest losses. Often their wealth was completely destroyed. The British poured into Nandi land like ants streaming into a house to eat sugar. When they got there, they took all the best grazing land. The first ones to arrive appropriated about 4,000 acres each. The next group took 3,000 acres and the last ones took about 2,000 acres. The Africans who really owned the land were told not to look for any more grass for their cattle. The British told them, 'Go sit in one place, don't move around because we own the land now. Furthermore, if you want to stay with us, you'll have to work for us. You may keep only five cattle, and the rest will have to go. You will be paid £2.50 a month.'

When the two grandmothers heard this, each one decided to make her own decision because of the seriousness of the matter. My step-grandmother asked, 'How many cattle will the British settler keep when he is asking you to keep five cattle?' and was told that the number would be 1,000 or more. She said that that was the worst deal she had ever heard of and she made up her mind instantly. She told her children, 'We aren't going to move from the land your father left us in. We are just going to die here, and you are not going to work for that terrible wage.'

They stayed on one of the reserves which the British set up but their cattle died of starvation because there wasn't sufficient land to support the herd and they became really poor. They had to learn how to make illegal alcohol to sell to live on. My step-grandma's life was miserable as she grew old; she never had enough to eat, she was always in trouble with her children because there was never enough of anything to go around, and the children were always fighting because of this. She had to drink alcohol, to eat chicken and eggs, and even to eat pork, which were all things that the older generation in my tribe didn't eat. It was very painful for my grandma to see her co-wife in trouble, and she tried to help her as much as she could.

My grandmother's decision was also very painful. She didn't like the idea of working on such miserable terms either, or of keeping only five cattle. Nor was she happy about dying one day on someone else's land. Finally she told her children to do anything they could to save their wealth. She said to them, 'Please don't mind about me or the land. I know I don't want to die on somebody else's land, but I can always stay with my brothers. They are farming their cattle out to other parts of the family so we will be all right.'

My father, her last-born, was a young man at the time. He had just married my mother, and at that point they had had only one child. My father didn't want to leave my grandmother with her brothers, and yet he wanted to explore. He dreamt of finding more grazing land. At that time people were pushing west, east, south and north to save their cattle either from being confiscated by the British or from dying of starvation. My father decided to marry another wife so that he could divide his cattle herd into two. He took his new wife with five cattle and went to work for the British on a farm. My mother was left to stay with my grandma and to look after the rest of the cattle. My father came to see them occasionally on weekends but he had to come a long way, about 50 miles on foot because nobody knew about cars in those days, or at least not in my family.

My mother said her life was very hard after my father moved away. She had to do all the jobs in the household such as taking care of the cattle and going to fetch firewood, and while she was struggling with all of that, she lost two of her children. She could no longer cope or look after the home well, and she became really sad. My father didn't know what had caused her children to die and felt my mother had neglected them. She decided she didn't want any more children but, as there were no methods of birth control in those days, she got pregnant anyway.

When my mother was five months pregnant, she asked my father to do something about the cattle because she wanted to join him and have the baby where he worked. Father said that if he took the cattle with him, the British would confiscate them and he couldn't leave them with Grandma Gogo on her own. When my mother realised that my father wasn't going to do anything for her, she stopped asking. When she was seven months pregnant she decided to go to have her baby at her mother's house. She got up one day and told my grandma she was going back to her home to have the baby there. Grandma asked her if she had discussed it with her husband. Mother said, 'No, my husband

doesn't want to discuss it, and I have made up my mind, I'm going.'
There was not much Grandma Gogo could say or do. She let her go.

The following week, after my mother had left, my father came to see
them. When he found out what my mother had done he was so angry
that he said that he never wanted to see my mother again as long as he
lived. He didn't have any choice this time, and he had to take his
mother and the cattle to the British farm with him whether he liked it
or not.

When they reached the farm he built a barn in the forest to hide the
new cattle. The farm was so big that it would have taken Mr Moore, the
owner, a month to go around it, but he didn't bother. Instead, he asked
the workers to keep a check on things, and they were always people like
my father, who had some extra cattle. They just told the British man
that the farm was fine. If Mr Moore ever decided to go around and
happened to find the cattle, that day would be the day you said
goodbye to the cattle.

While my father was worrying about these matters, my mother was
at her home taking it easy waiting for her baby to come. She had heard
that my father never wanted to see her again and thought that that was
actually a pretty good idea, considering how hard life was with him.
She stayed until the baby was born, and that baby was me. She tried to
find a relative of my father to give me a name. She found one, and I was
given a name but it was wrong.

The way to identify which of two people who shared the same spirit
name in the past has been reincarnated is to ask the child you are giving
the name to. For example, we are three Tapsubeis now, and if we are all
dead when the spirit's name comes back to a child, the person who is
giving the name will ask it which Tapsubei it is.

'Are you Tapsubei, Mrs Creider, the mother of Colin?'

If the child was me then it would show a sign. If not, the attempt to
find out would continue until the right one was found.

So what happened to me was that they identified the wrong person.
My mother said that after two days I was so sick that there was nothing
they could do to help me. They tried every kind of medicine, but I
didn't get any better. At last Grandmother Chesanga, my mother's
mother, told her to take me back to my father's home. They said that I
had gone blind and that sickness had almost destroyed me. As soon as
my mother got to my father's house, Grandmother Gogo asked her

what spirit name she had called me. Mother told her that I was named Chepituny. (Chepituny was the reincarnation name of the woman who was later to be called Tapsubei, but also the name of another woman.) Grandma took me and put me in her lap. She told me to be happy and to sleep well. 'I know you already,' she said. They said I went to sleep as though nothing were wrong with me. The next morning Grandma Gogo brought some milk and a dry red clay for use in a ritual. She looked for some green grass and made a stopper which she put in the top of the gourd holding the milk.

Grandmother asked my mother which Chepituny I was named after.

'Mrs Kitegoi,' my mother said.

Grandma said to me, 'But I know you are Chepituny Tapsubei, Mrs Surai, the mother of Marat Chok.' They said that right then I gave a good sign that I accepted the spirit name I had been given (because that's who I was). After that I was fine and had no health problems.

After the problem of who I was had been solved, Grandma Gogo discussed the problem of my mother and father. She told them that they should forgive each other and live together because it was not good for me to be taken away from my home. Father quickly agreed because he believed that no child of his should be raised outside the family. He especially thought that no child should be raised in my mother's family. My father didn't like them because when the missionaries came to Nandi country to tell people to believe in God, my mother's family were the first to be converted. In fact, only one great-uncle and his family became Christians but, because our society values tradition very highly, this one person affected the whole family's reputation badly. Although my mother knew what my father thought of her family, she agreed to stay with him. Or at least she tried.

Now the two wives had to stay together in the same house. The family had become very large because some of my father's brothers had moved to our house to stay while they looked for work. Everyone was together during the day, cooking and eating in one place, but at night most of the guests had to go and look elsewhere for a place to sleep. The house was divided in two. The sheep and goats slept in one side and the people lived in the other. There was so little space in our part that my mother had to sleep with the sheep and goats. She said that she put me against the wall so that the animals wouldn't step on me during the night. She herself slept beside the livestock with a long stick to push the animals away when they crowded near us.

Mother complained that my father was lazy and didn't think of building another house; he didn't like working for the British man, and yet he didn't have any other plans. Often he would stay at home and get his brother to replace him, saying that he was sick.

One day it was very late when he told his brother to go to work for him and when my uncle reached the British man, he was asked where my father was. My uncle said that he was sick. Mr Moore asked him why he came to work so late then. My uncle said that my father didn't tell him he was sick until very late. The farmer didn't accept this explanation, and he ordered my uncle to lie down and be whipped. My uncle said to him, 'Not on your life will I lie down for you to whip me.'

He ran off as fast as he could towards home with the farmer running after him. When my uncle looked back he saw Mr Moore was still chasing him. He ran as fast as he could. Mother said that she was making lunch when suddenly someone burst in the front door and ran to where I had been put to sleep. Mother asked him, 'What? What is chasing you?'

He couldn't answer. He was shaking and trembling so much that he could hardly put his feet on the ground. Mother dashed to the front door and peeped out. She saw Mr Moore running towards her like a madman. The wind was blowing his hair so that it looked like a lion's mane. In his left hand he was carrying his rifle and in his right hand he had a whip.

When mother saw that, she thought something dreadful was going to happen. Maybe he would shoot her. But nothing could be worse than his stepping on her sleeping child. She ran to the fireplace, grabbed a burning log and then turned back to meet the intruder. When she got to the door, she hit him right away before he got any further. She got him by surprise, and he reeled away. He wasn't prepared for anyone who would challenge him. He thought that as soon as the people saw him they would run flying through the back door. He went home and sent a person to tell my father to see him.

My father thought that he probably wanted to whip him too, so he got ready. He told my mother, 'The British man has called me. I guess he wants to whip me, but I won't let him do that to me, if I have to die with him. However, it will depend on who gets who first.'

When he got to the house the man was waiting outside. He called my father, 'Kipserem!'

'Yes, *bwana mkubwa*?' my father said. (That means 'Yes, Mr Big?')

'I want your brother to leave this farm right away. I don't want to see him here again, and if I do, I'll shoot him.'

'Yes, sir,' my father said. He went back home and told his brother what Mr Moore had said. The two brothers laughed, and then my uncle said, 'It is for the best; I didn't like him anyway.'

The Nandi people then were amazing (and they still are). They wouldn't do what you asked them to do if they decided you had the wrong personality for their taste. That is what happened to the British with my people on the farms. My people were completely fed up with them. They watched the British as though they were clowns playing with children. And they listened to them as though they were listening to a radio singing in a language that no one understands. Nandi are not people who like to argue. They just watch you to see what kind of person you are and then, if they like you, they will treat you just like one of them. But if they think you are odd, they will make up a name which will match your character. For example 'Termite' for a person who likes to knife you little by little until you fall apart. The British were called 'Tornado' (which lifts up your house and leaves you without a shelter).

Although the British were bad, my father still managed to struggle with them a little longer. It was difficult for the two mothers because they had to stay in the house together. Two women married to one man living in the same house is impossible. It is not bad for the children, but it is for the wives. One wife will try to 'capture' the husband by doing anything he asks. Even if he says that he has somewhere to go at five in the morning the next day, the wife who is trying to be good will get up at four and make tea for him. The other wife will be the one who gets beaten if anything goes wrong. The husband won't talk to her for days and days. Eventually such a woman can be shunted to one side and only visited by the husband for the purpose of providing her with children.

My mother was not the kind to curry favour with anyone. She knew what kind of life she wanted to live and she wouldn't let anyone push her around. If her husband said that he was going somewhere in the morning, she would say, 'Fine, I'll see you when you come back.' She wouldn't get up and make tea unless she was asked to. If the husband didn't like the tea she made she said, 'All right.' She didn't ask him if he would like her to make something different for him.

My father, on the other hand, came from a family which considered themselves royalty. If they said anything, it should be attended to. The two of them were really alike because they were both powerful personalities.

They just couldn't live together, and when I was one year old, my mother took me back to her mother's and went to look for a job to support herself and me.

She wanted me to go to school very much. She knew the world would never go back to the way it used to be and she wanted her child to be able to do anything a European could do. It didn't matter to her whether it was a girl or a boy; she wanted her children to be equal. She worked and saved money to put me into school. When I was four years old, she took me to a mission school near Grandma Chesanga's house. It was a little place, mainly used to teach people about God, but in the morning it was used for little children. I went there for a year.

The second year, a message reached my father from people who were travelling that his child had been taken to mission school. He thought that that was terrible.

'How could that woman do that to my child? How could she get her mixed up in such a way? I must go to rescue her.'

'No,' Grandmother Gogo said. "You can't go and bring the child without the mother. You may go and bring them both, but it's not right to let the child be raised by a stepmother if her mother is still alive.'

'No,' Father said. 'I don't want the mother any more, and I'm not going to bring the child for anyone else to raise. I'm going to bring her to raise by myself the way I want.'

'It's up to you,' Grandma Gogo said, 'but what you are doing is against my wish.'

'It doesn't matter,' my father said.

So he came to get me. He had to travel about 80 miles, and the journey took him two days. When he arrived he didn't go to Grandma Chesanga's house because he didn't want my mother to know he was there. When the neighbours found out that he wanted to take me they sent a secret message telling my mother to hide me. Mother didn't waste any time. She took me straight away to her cousin's house.

The next day father went to see her. The house was very quiet because only Grandma Chesanga was there. Father asked about me. Grandma said that she didn't know where we were, that we had left at night while she was still asleep. Father was very disappointed, but he knew that my mother hadn't gone far away. He started looking in all the houses in the vicinity, but without success. Meantime, my mother had hidden me in a cave near Grandma Chesanga's house. She climbed up on a hill to see if my father was looking for us. Her only hope was that my father would only search the houses for me and not look outside. But my father started looking everywhere. He had in fact been told that my mother was still around. At twelve noon my mother decided to go to look for something to eat in Grandma Chesanga's house. We had been in the cave all morning without food and I was beginning to cry from hunger. Mother was afraid to take me so she left me alone in the cave. I suppose I was afraid of the dark, and I came out of the cave crying, a scared little girl. Father heard my voice and guessed that I was his child. He came to the cave with two men, my mother's uncle and my mother's cousin. Every person in that neighbourhood was related to my mother, but despite that they couldn't fight for her to keep me because that was not allowed by our customs.

Mother came running back bringing a pail of corn. As she reached the cave she saw me in my father's arms. I still remember hearing her cry, 'Oh no, you are not going to take my child away from me.'

'Tell that woman to stay away from here or she is going to get it,' my father ordered the two men. They told my mother to give up because nothing could be done.

'After all the child is his, and if he wants to look after it by himself without a mother it is all right. Don't fight for her. Let him take her.'

There was nothing my mother could do to keep me with her. It felt so bad having to leave my mother. There is nothing that can happen as bad as that, and it still frightens me to think about it. When I do I feel that someone is going to make me a little child again and then make me go through the same experience. I didn't know my father at all. I knew I had a father, but I had never seen him before that day when he took me.

I remember crying all the way on the journey back. Whenever my father put me down so that he could rest, I would try to run to look for my mother. I tried to fight too. I remember that when my father put me on his shoulder I tried to bite him and asked him to take me back to my mother.

It took us two days to get to my father's home, and on the way we stayed with one of my father's cousin's. The food was very different. There was milk and *ugali* (a stiff porridge made from maize-meal). I took one bit of *ugali* and one swallow of milk, and that was it. I took all the *ugali* that I was supposed to eat and slipped it through the partition into the room where the sheep and goats slept. I drank the milk only. People were amazed at how much I ate. Finally they asked me if I was finished, and I said yes.

In the morning when the lady of the house opened the door to let the sheep out she found the *ugali*. She said no wonder we thought the child ate very fast. Father said that when they asked me why I threw the *ugali* away, I told them that it tasted as though I was eating mud with warts. In the morning they gave me milk again for breakfast. More trouble. At my mother's we had eaten bread sometimes with tea or just tea alone. I had never seen anyone drink milk alone for breakfast. We left that morning, and father carried me all the way home.

CHAPTER THREE
Life on a British Farm

We got home in the evening. Everybody was at home when we got there: my stepmother, her two children, a babysitter, a shepherd, and my father's mother, Grandmother Gogo. Everybody in the house gathered around wanting to talk to me. I spoke with a different accent, and none of the other children would say anything at all.

As the days went by I learned to like Grandmother Gogo best of all in the family, and I made some new friends. My best friend was Mrs Kimobo an old lady who lived in our neighbourhood. I got along well with my half-brother, Kipsang, too. He was my age, and his sister was two years younger. We played together and looked after sheep. I liked my baby sister. I used to call her imaginary names, and I liked to sleep beside her at night. I began having a good time. Grandma spoiled me because she came every morning to take me and my brother to her house. We were free there, especially me because I had a problem drinking milk. I didn't like it: what I wanted was yogurt. When I was in Grandma Gogo's house I was free to say what I liked and what I didn't like.

Our house was built up on a little hill, and in the rear of the house there was a ditch to carry the urine of the sheep and goats away, and because of Mau Mau trouble we also used this little ditch. By the afternoon, with the sun heating the urine, when we played tag around the house, I remember that my eyes would burn from the ammonia smell when I had to jump over the ditch. If I stepped in it, I would carry my foot around for hours as though it had been wounded. As soon as I got a chance, I would wash and wash the foot to get it clean. This was because my mother's people didn't keep livestock in their house, and so I wasn't used to it. My stepmother and brothers and sisters really used to laugh at me for this.

Two years after my return the country was in trouble because of the

Mau Mau uprising. This was a terrorist movement led by the Kikuyu tribe to try and force the British to give them back their land. The Kikuyu attacked the British in their homes and in retaliation the British arrested the Kikuyu and detained them in concentration camps. We lived with many Kikuyu people on the farm. They weren't cattle-keepers, but they worked in the cornfields of the British farmers. I had some Kikuyu children as friends because we were living in the same neighbourhood, and I was a friendly child, but my father was unhappy about this. He tried to keep me from going to play with those children because it was very dangerous; the Kikuyus could be captured at any time without any warning and my father was afraid that someday I would be captured as well. Grandma was given the job of being my watchdog.

We lived in mud houses with roofs of grass thatching. The door was made of pieces of wood which were sealed together at night. Since we didn't have any bathroom in the house, we had to go out to urinate at six o'clock and after that no one would let us eat or drink so that we wouldn't have to go out at night.

Today's children seem to me to be very clever even when they are very young. We were pretty slow when we were growing up. Maybe this was because we had only our parents to learn from. There was no television. Our parents wouldn't tell us things they thought were bad for the children to know. For example, during the Mau Mau war, if we had had a television, we would have known much more about it, and maybe we would have been frightened and stayed away from the Kikuyu children.

I have never forgotten the day Kikuyu people were captured in a nearby camp. Some were captured with all of their children, but others didn't have time to see to their children's safety. The police just kicked in their doors at night and got them in their sleep. The poor person would only be able to grab the children nearby; sometimes two or more would be left in the house.

After the people in the camp next to us were captured, a friend of mine found three children who had been left behind. They were so hungry that they were trying to eat the soil. The younger one couldn't chew the earth, so the older one was trying to mix the soil with water. My friend came and told me, 'I've found some children who are eating dirt. It seems that they don't have any parents. They could be our children, mine and yours, if you want to have some.'

'Yes,' I said, 'I want some children.'

I told my grandma that I was going to play with this Nandi girl outside and my friend told her mother that she wanted to play with me. When we reached the children they were still eating earth. We took them to a place near our houses by a little river. We tried to play with them but they were so hungry they were eating anything in sight including wild fruit. For us fruit was poisonous and we were worried because we couldn't stop them. Finally we realised they were hungry. My friend was only one year older than me, but she knew so much more than I did. She told me to go and ask my grandmother for food.

'When she gives it to you, tell her you want to eat it outside with me. Then you can bring it here for these children.'

I went home to ask for food. Grandma gave me enough food for two people and I ran as fast as I could. When the children saw the food we could see the joy in their eyes. They ran to gather round me. I gave them the food, and they ate it so fast that by the time my girlfriend got back with more food, they had already finished what I had given them. After they had eaten the second portion of food, the children began to be happy. They started playing and began becoming attached to us. We played with them until four in the afternoon when we suddenly realised that we had to go home. We both knew that nobody would let us keep the children for fear that we would be captured. So my girlfriend said, 'Let us build a little grass house.'

We hoped that after we had built the house the children would stay there and we could come at night and keep an eye on them. We started to cut grass and gather tree leaves to build the house but we realised we had to find food for them for the night. I told her Grandma Gogo wouldn't let me take food out again.

'No,' she said, 'you are not going to ask your grandma then.'

I asked her how I was going to get it.

'We just have to steal it, and when they ask about it, we'll say we ate it.'

My friend went to her home to look for food, and I went to mine. I ran outside to see if my grandma was coming. I looked around and spotted her looking for firewood. I ran back in, took my cup and climbed the ladder. I looked and looked, and finally I saw a container of sugar in the corner. I filled my cup and came down but as I reached the door, my grandma arrived. She called me to come help her take the firewood in. I looked very suspicious to her.

'What do you have in your cup?' she asked me.

'Sugar,' I said.

'Sugar?' she repeated.

'Yes,' I said.

'How did you get it, and where are you taking it?'

I told her I had got it from the attic and that I was taking it to our children.

'Our children,' she chuckled, 'your children and whose?'

'My children and my girlfriend's', I said.

She took me by the hand and said, 'Let's go. Show me your children.'

When we got there my girlfriend was there already giving food to the children. Grandma was scared when she saw them; she had assumed they were toy children.

Grandma called the mother of my girlfriend to ask her what they should do with the children. She said that the children had to be returned to where we found them. She told my grandma that it was very dangerous to keep them and that there was no chance of our staying alive if we kept them.

'If the British don't capture you with them someday, then the Kikuyu may find you and kill you and take the children away.'

Both women didn't like to see the children taken back to the empty camp, but they had to. They prepared food for the children and then, hiding behind the trees, we took the children back to the camp.

That was the last time we ever saw them. I hope they survived. Their only hope of survival was to be found by a Nandi policeman. I discovered later that Nandi policemen saved a lot of Kikuyu children's lives because I met a lot of Kikuyu children being raised with Nandi families as I grew up.

Living with the British was not easy. People were not sure of their lives any longer, because the British farmer could ask you at any time to move from his land, which is just what happened to my father one day.

He went to work one morning, and when he got there Mr Moore told him he was late. He told him to lie down to be whipped. Father lay down, but as soon as he reached the ground he changed his mind and said to himself, 'I won't let him touch me like the others.' He turned quickly and kicked the farmer who fell down. Instantly my father grabbed him, before he even had a chance to breathe, and bit him. He bit his finger so hard that he bit it right off.

That almost cost my father his life. The farmer blew his whistle; this was a signal that there was serious trouble. People ran to them from every direction. The farmer was still struggling with my father even though he was bleeding badly. The people separated them, and the farmer ordered the police to be called right away. He said that he wanted my father hung or put away for good.

When the police arrived they asked my father if he had anything to tell his family because that might be the last time he would see them. Father was brought home by the police, his hands tied behind his back and blood all over his clothes. I was very scared when I saw the blood because I thought someone had tried to kill him. Grandma was inside. The police called her, and as soon as she came out and saw my father, she started crying, 'My child, oh my child!' My stepmother was called too and came crying. The police were in a hurry and told my father to say what he had to say quickly.

Father told Grandma Gogo to look after me and not to let my mother take me away, no matter what. He told my stepmother that he didn't know if he would ever come back and to look after herself. And that was it. My grandmother gave my father a last glass of milk, and there was no time for anything more. The police took him away. We children cried as much as we could, but that didn't change a thing.

We found out about that my father was to appear in court through the police, who were Nandi. They knew my father and respected him. When they had finished work they would come over to our home if they had any news. The case went on for six months, and during the whole affair our family was kept abreast of what was happening by the police. Finally my father was sentenced to prison for two years with six strokes of the whip every two weeks. That was better than being hung or put in prison for ever, so when the police came with that news everyone was greatly relieved, although the whipping was very bad.

When my mother heard that father was in jail, she came to try and take me back. When I met her, she seemed like a stranger and I told her I couldn't leave without my grandmother.

When I said that to my mother, her feelings were deeply hurt, and she walked away without saying goodbye. She left for good, and never tried to take me back again. She didn't want to force me even though she was upset. I was unaware of her pain, and just felt happy that she didn't make me leave Grandma Gogo.

We continued to live with my grandmother's brother until my father got out of jail. I still remember when he came back. He didn't come home right away, but first had to undergo a ceremony to cleanse him from the unclean things he had done in jail. For example, when one of the inmates died, the other prisoners had to bury him. Also he may have cleaned latrines. These are things which are considered bad for a Nandi to do, and I think that must have been the reason for the ceremony. No one ever told us children why the ceremony was being done; I just happened to overhear Grandma Gogo talking about it. The Nandi people have a custom of not telling their children what is happening. Older people are very careful about what they say to their children and insist on a lot of privacy.

After my father was clean, he came home. My stepmother and grandmother were crying for joy, but as for us, we didn't see anything to cry for. I guess we didn't know how bad it was when he was away.

Two months after he returned, my father came to a decision. He had learned that people were emigrating to a new land where another tribe, called the Luyia, lived. Father was determined that he would never work for the British again as long as he lived, and he told Grandma Gogo that he wanted to emigrate. That was terrible for me because it meant I had to leave Grandma behind and I was only nine years old. I would miss her dreadfully.

The Luyia country was a very scary place to go. Because there were a lot of mosquitoes, it was particularly dangerous for children. When we left, Grandma Gogo was very sad at the thought that we might not all come back. We walked for almost three weeks until we got to a place called Cheboiwa. We had left Nandi country 30 miles behind and were now in a completely different land. The trees and vegetation, the people and their language and food were all different. In the morning, the sun would come over the mountain to the east and would shine over us so that places to the west would be sparkling while we were still in shade. In the evening, the sun would stay with us while it was dark further west. A little breeze would pass through making the leaves of the trees shimmer. Monkey families would come out on the rocks to catch the last of the day's sun and sit and chatter with one another.

We stayed with a Nandi man who had been there for three years while my father looked around for a place to build a house. The country was very crowded with people, but none of them had cattle. When a Nandi man came everybody wanted him to live with them in order to get oxen to plough their fields. Everyone asked my father 'Do you have any oxen?' and he got a place right away because he had a lot of cattle. A house was built immediately, and we moved into it.

My half-brother Kipsang and I were the older children, so we had to look after the cattle.

There were only two other Nandi families in the area, both with children. Whenever we met them we would ask them why the people of that land didn't understand Nandi.

'I wonder if they are really people,' I said. 'They have eyes; they walk, eat, and wear clothes; so what do you think might have happened to them that they don't understand Nandi?'

Two of the Nandi children were twins, and when we asked them this, they said that they didn't know what had happened to the people. The older twin said, 'I have proved that they don't understand Nandi. I sometimes say to them, "Hello, mouse", and they just say hello back. You can prove it for yourself if you want to. We can wait for someone in the road and say, "Hello, mouse", and you'll see.'

We waited, and in a minute a man walked past. The girl said, 'Hello, mouse', and the man said, 'Hello'.

I was so sad because he seemed to be a real person. In my mind, anyone who was not a Nandi was not a real human being. I would always feel pity for such people.

Kipsang was not interested in knowing a lot about these people, but sometimes he came up with some wonderings too. One day he asked me, 'Do you think these people have a problem eating the way we do?'

I told him that I thought it would be a good thing to find out.

'If you are going to find out,' he told me, 'also see if they sleep like us.'

The next day I asked the twins because they had been in Luyia country for a long time and even understood the language, whether the Luyia people ate like us.

'No,' one twin said, 'they eat differently from us.'

'How?' I asked, 'don't they eat with their mouths?'

The girl said that they ate with their mouths all right, but that their food was very different. They ate sweet potatoes, green vegetables, cassava, maize-meal porridge, fish, and they ate everything with water. A lot of the foods she mentioned I didn't even know about. I quickly asked what fish was.

'A fish is a small snake. They get it from the water alive, kill it, cook it and eat it with porridge.'

'Oh no!' I let out a horrified gasp. 'Snakes!'

When the girl finished telling me about the food, I thought that these people were in very serious trouble. I also began to be afraid of them because I had never heard of anyone who ate snakes.

The day was ending, and we took the cattle home to be milked. I was very excited about telling my father what I had learned but Kipsang said to me, 'You don't really believe what we were told today do you?'

He thought that the girl was making it up.

'No,' I said, 'I think she's right.'

I told father that I had come to tell him about what the people in this country ate. He laughed and told me to tell him.

'I'm afraid that when you hear this you will want to go back where Grandma is tomorrow,' I told him very seriously. 'I don't think you know that they eat something called fish. A fish is a kind of snake from the water. They also eat the roots of a tree called cassava, and they boil bananas when they are still raw to eat.'

I gave my father the whole list of foods that the people ate, and he listened and laughed his head off. Although he was laughing at me, he himself hadn't heard of half the foods either. He was able, however, to help me with the worst one, because he had at least heard about fish. He tried to explain, but since he didn't know what to call it himself, he had to call it a 'snake from the water' also. He told me that it was only food for the Luyia people, and that it was not good for a Nandi person so I must never try to eat one.

My stepmother had never heard of fish in her life. She persisted in asking me how big I had been told they were. All I could say was that they were the size of snakes. She was more terrified than I was. She said that I was absolutely never to eat anything from anyone's house as long as we lived in that country.

It didn't take me long to realise that my parents didn't know very much about the Luyia. I eagerly became a newspaper for my parents, and everything I heard I would tell them. They were always curious to hear. After we had been there for three months, they still had exactly the same set of friends that they had had when we arrived – the other Nandi. But it was easy for us children to make friends, and after three months we had found friends from all sorts of tribes. We had Masai children for friends, Mt Elgon Masai (Kony people), Sebei, Teso and Luyia. The children of the Masai that lived there (called Kibwobek) were just like us. We played with them often, and we knew that they spoke my grandma's language.

The children that we were most fascinated by were the Elgon Masai and the Sebei. They spoke a language which was almost like Nandi, but with a very strong accent and with many different words. They were also a little like the Luyia in their customs and character. I decided to call them half-and-half Nandi because anything that they said was half Nandi and half their own language. I tried so hard to teach them to speak like us. I felt sorry for them a lot and would say to myself, 'Poor people, they have such problems; they can't talk like real people.'

One day I asked some of the children we were playing with, 'How do you eat? Do you have a problem eating because of your accent?'

'No,' they said to me, 'we eat just fine.'

'Let's pick some fruit and share it with them to see if they eat it like us,' my brother said to me.

We picked the fruit, a sour, lemon-like fruit and sat together and ate it. I didn't see anything different about the way they ate the fruit, but my brother was sure he saw a difference. He said that for one thing, when one of them ate he could see the earring shaking in her ears, and for another thing, they talked when they had food in their mouths (something we wouldn't do). The earring must have been shaking because of the sourness of the fruit. My parents had taught us not to talk when we ate, and so when we saw anyone eat who hadn't been taught in this way, we assumed they were different from us.

After we had lived there for three years, more Nandi people arrived who were running away from the British. The place where we lived belonged to a Luyia people called the Kabras. Six Nandi families remained in Kabras with us. We had more children to play with and with whom we could keep up our traditions. Some people moved very close to our house and we could sleep with them. We especially liked an old woman who told us stories when we slept in her house. We were five girls, all between the ages of eight and eleven, and there were three boys. We all slept in the same house with the old woman, but she gave a strict warning to the boys to not bother us at night.

We were very old-fashioned when we lived in this Luyia country because everything we knew was taught to us by our parents. The songs we sang were taught to us by the old lady, and they were the songs she used to sing when she was young. We could only learn the songs which were current when some visitors with children came and brought us up to date. Then we would stay with the same songs until other visitors with children arrived.

CHAPTER FOUR
Ceremonies and Adventures

In 1957, when I must have been eleven years old, my uncle came to invite my family to a circumcision ceremony for my cousin Christina Cheptarus. Father said that he wanted me to go to the ceremony with my stepmother so that I could see what Nandi people looked like when they dressed up for ceremonies. I went with my stepmother on foot and it took us four days to get there. We reached the border of Luyia country in one day, and after that we were in Nandi country. Father gave us a list of the places where we were to sleep on the way.

The fourth day we were really tired. By the afternoon we had reached a river called the Pirei. The river was not easy to see. There was a lot of swampy grass which grew very tall, and the way could appear dry on the surface but be deep and dangerous underneath.

It was very difficult to walk in the swamp and my stepmother tried to show me how. I had never been in a swamp like that before and I didn't see what there was to worry about. She asked me if I had understood what she had showed me. I said yes, but in my mind I was also thinking, 'What's so hard about this if I can see the grass?'

'Let's go,' my stepmother said, and she went ahead of me.

As soon as I set my foot down hard in the water, the swamp felt like it was swallowing my foot.

'It's swallowing my foot,' I cried out.

'Move, don't just stand there,' she said. 'You must move quickly so your foot doesn't sink in.'

The swamp was shaking like jello. When I moved the whole swamp shook around me, and the further I went, the more the swamp seemed to be swallowing my feet. We went about 20 feet until we got to the middle of the swamp. My stepmother told me to jump. I jumped, but I couldn't make it. One foot slipped, I dropped the blanket I was carrying and grabbed the grass. I cried for help. My stepmother turned back and said, 'All right, hang on, I'm coming.'

She came back and told me to give her my hand. I was afraid to let go of the grass because I thought I would drown. Even though I was holding on to the grass, my feet were sinking endlessly. The water was up to my waist. I was about to give up when my stepmother bent down and took my hand. She had the baby on her back, but something gave her strength, and she pulled me out.

I hadn't cried when I was drowning, but after I was rescued I began to think I was going to die. I cried all the way. Even after we had reached our destination I continued to cry. My stepmother didn't cry, but she was very frightened. She thought that if I had drowned, my father would never have forgiven her. That night we were very tired. My cousins brought water from a well, boiled it and let us wash our feet with it. After we had finished, we ate and went to bed exhausted.

The girl for whom the ceremony was being held was still travelling around inviting more and more relatives. The big event was two weeks away. Many more guests arrived including some relatives from Kapkures where my real mother lived. They spent time with me telling me about my mother and my half-brothers. Now that I was old enough to know what the word mother really meant, I had a lot of questions: Does mother love me? Does she remember me? What do the other children look like? Do they know they have a sister? The relatives had a lot to ask me, too. They asked me if I would like to go with them to see my mother. I wanted to, but I was afraid of my father. I was hoping my mother would come to the ceremony so that I could see her; I had no memory of what she looked like.

We were expecting Christina any day now, and I was very excited about the whole thing. I was looking forward especially to seeing the leg bells she was going to wear. When children are being initiated both they and the officers of the ceremony dress in special clothing. The officers wear traditional skin clothing, and the girls wear very elaborate costumes given them by their boyfriends. Because of this the costumes consist of many items of a warrior's outfit: various kinds of bells, an elaborate head-dress, leglets, apron and shoulder pieces of long monkey fur, and so on.

Christina arrived at midnight and I was already asleep. Although the women were drunk, they rushed outside when they heard the bells sounding and the whistles blowing as she came. The noise woke me up, and as soon as I heard the sound, I knew that the girl and her entourage had arrived. My cousin Chemonos, her sister, was up too, and she called me, 'Tapsubei, are you awake?' When I said that I was, she said, 'Let's go out to meet her.'

As soon as my cousin, the one who was going to be initiated, saw me, she ran to hug me and shake my hand. She was very happy to see me. We looked a lot alike, and her parents had told her she looked like me. She stared at me, and I stared at her. The girls were very tired because they had walked about 40 miles a day inviting relatives to the ceremony. There were six girls who were going to be initiated together.

They were so exhausted they couldn't sing that night even though the women were insisting that they sing for their fathers. They took off their bells and gave them to the younger girls like us to sing for the old men. The older girls made up the chorus, while we danced and sang.

Each of the girls was going to see her boyfriend. They had only two weeks before they changed from girls into women. They needed all the time they could get to be with their boyfriends, because some of them would not be able to marry their boyfriends. Often girls wanted to marry their boyfriends, but were not able to do so because their parents decided differently.

I learned a lot when I was there: to sing a new song, to put bells on my legs and how to dance. I was looking forward to going back to teach the other children at home. I appeared very old-fashioned to the children who had gathered for the ceremony. I had had my ears pierced, I was wearing long clothes, and my hair was always cut short. After I had been there for three days, my cousin dressed me nicely in her own clothes; she didn't need them any longer, because once she was initiated she would wear different ones.

On the night of the initiation the girls danced and distributed cigarettes. I didn't see where they got them from. Each girl had two girls who worked for her: one girl took the cigarettes out of the package, and the other girl lit them. The girl who was being initiated gave the cigarette away after it had been lit. She was giving them out to everybody, even to me. I didn't smoke of course, and I had no idea of what to do with a cigarette but I didn't want her to know. I thought that the others would laugh at me even more because they already thought I was old-fashioned. Whenever I got a cigarette, I gave it to my stepmother.

We danced all night long. The following morning the girls distributed all their gifts. They gave gifts to their boyfriends and close relatives. My cousin gave me a cup, a glass, a packet of cigarettes, some sweets, and a bottle of soda. That was the happiest day of my life. The packet of cigarettes I was given had a picture of a crowned crane, one of the most majestic and beautiful birds in Africa. I didn't want anyone to open the cigarettes, because I liked looking at the picture so much.

We stayed on after the ceremony until my cousin was engaged and then we left. I hated to leave because I had to leave the people who knew my mother. On the other hand I was very excited to go back home to teach the other children what I had learned. We walked home again, but it was not so bad going back. We took a long road so that we didn't have to go through the swamp again. We stayed with my father's first cousin on the last night of the journey. There was one girl who was older than me and who was going to boarding school. She had a lot of clothes; I was amazed at how many articles of clothing she had whilst I didn't even have any underwear. I had only the one dress my cousin had given me and one skirt with a little bandana which I tied around my neck. She took me to her room to show me her things, and she told me what she did in school. They were Catholics, and she told me how to pray and taught me a hymn sung in church. But my mind was not in the mood to understand about church songs or prayers. I asked after she had finished teaching me, 'How many underpants do you have?'

'I have five pairs,' she said to me. 'How many do you have?'

I didn't have any.

'You mean you wear clothes without underwear?' she said.

'Yes,' I said, 'I don't wear any underwear because they are very hard to find where I come from.' I didn't want her to think that I was old-fashioned and didn't know about underwear, but the fact was I didn't know that girls wore such things. I used to think that they were for boys only, because where I came from boys wore short pants and girls wore skirts. Before we left the next day I was careful to tell the girl how amazed I was that she had so much underwear. She said she would like to give me a pair. 'Let's go and see if I have your size.'

Oh my! I was so happy I was just smiling and couldn't even close my mouth. She gave me an orange pair with a little pocket on the back. I put them on right away in her bedroom. I wanted to take my skirt off so people could see them. Then they would know that I had underpants too! When my cousin saw what I was going to do, she told me, 'Oh no, you wear the underpants inside your other clothes.' I was dying to get home to show the other children what I had.

When I got home all the children wanted to see me. I had brought back sweets for them, and they all gathered round me. They asked me what Nandi country looked like. I told them that it looked good, and I told them that Nandi children smoked something called cigarettes. They all asked me what they were. I took out the prized packet and showed it to them.

'What is this?' they said. 'How do you smoke it?'

I told them that the packet had to be opened and one cigarette had to be lit, but that I wanted to wait for all my friends to come before I opened the packet. I showed them my underpants. They were very excited and each one asked me if he or she could try them on. I said sure, and took them off. Everyone tried them on, even my littlest sister, except my brother who said that he didn't want to wear girls' clothes, so he didn't try them on.

My friends arrived at seven-thirty, and the first thing my sisters said was that now I had to open my cigarettes. I explained to them what they were first. I took one cigarette out but none of us knew how to smoke. Father's new wife, a Sebei woman who had grown up on a British farm, had often seen smoking so she showed us. We tried, but each person coughed a great deal. We left them and I put them away for safe-keeping in the attic.

I told my brother and sisters and friends how the girls had danced and how many places we had been to with them. I told them about the swamp we had crossed. They were all impatient to learn the new songs I had come back with, so I taught them one. I was feeling very sophisticated now because I had a dress, a skirt and a pair of underpants.

I was looking forward to going to sleep in the house of Mrs Salei, an old woman, the next day. We always told her before she went to bed to wake us up at seven in the morning. I had to get up at that time because I needed to get my own milk. My two friends got up then too, because like me they didn't have their own mother and had to do their own milking. I had both a good time and a bad time in those days. For one thing, my father was a very fierce man, and if we children did something bad we would be punished severely. Sometimes we wished we had never been born into that house. I was the one who especially got punished because I was the one who looked after the cattle. This was a difficult task. There were a lot of cattle – about 80. There were also about 20 sheep which I had to take care of. My brother used to help me, but now he had gone to school and I had only my seven-year-old sister. I myself was only eleven. The Luyia people were very sensitive. If cattle ate even the tiniest bit of their corn, they would scream as though someone had died. Of course my sister was punished too, but she was very young and there is a limit to how much you can punish a seven-year-old.

I never knew how my stepmother felt about me because she was a quiet woman. It was impossible to know if she was angry or not because she kept her feelings inside. She never told me she didn't like this or that when I was with her. One rainy evening when I returned from looking after the cattle I found my father and my stepmother arguing about me. They would have liked to stop when they saw me, but they were arguing so fiercely they couldn't. That was the day that I knew how bad it was not to have your own mother to look after you. The row had started because my father had said to my stepmother, 'Tapsubei shouldn't go to milk the cattle today because she has been in the rain all day long and must be very cold.'

Stepmother didn't like that at all. She asked my father, 'Why do you worry about this child more than my children? Do you think I beat her? You never get her to help me grind maize-meal. You never get her to sweep the house for me, and she never carries water for me. Why do I do all these other things for her? I'm not her mother.'

Father was really angry. He told my stepmother that she should be happy with what I did. I looked after the cattle and babysat at the same time. He said that he had taught me to milk cattle when I was only seven years old so that she wouldn't have to do it.

'I never want to see you doing anything other than looking after the cattle, the baby, milking your own milk, and washing your own dishes,' my father said to me. 'If your mother doesn't want to give you food, you can drink milk. Milk is better for you anyway, and besides, I can always eat with you.'

Then my father turned back to my stepmother. 'You don't have to worry for the sake of your own children that if you don't work they won't have enough to eat,' he told her. 'Why do you drink milk with your children, but neither you nor your children look after the cattle?' He said that he thought it was a mistake for me to look after the cattle because I was alone.

'She doesn't have any sisters or brothers. She is really working for you, because you are the one who has the children.'

The argument had got so bad that I left because I didn't want to listen any more. I went to hide. When they finished arguing my stepmother came out to milk and then went to feed her children. I heard them call me to come to eat. I didn't answer. I was afraid to go in; I thought that if I did they would start again. I heard my father call me but I didn't answer. He went in and I heard him say, 'She will come when it gets cold.'

I was waiting for the light to go off so I could go to the granary to sleep. My father kept coming out to call me but finally he gave up. I didn't have anything to cover myself with in the granary but I was very tired and had no trouble getting to sleep. I planned to get up early the next day but I overslept in the morning. Father found me in the morning but didn't want to wake me up. He waited until I woke up by myself.

I woke up thinking I was in the house. I had forgotten about being in the granary. I asked myself, 'What's happened? Why am I sleeping on top of the corn?' Then suddenly I remembered that I had run away the night before. I tried to sneak out slowly, but my father was sitting right outside.

'What have you been doing all morning long in this granary?' he said to me. 'Don't you think you should get ready to milk your cattle?'

'Yes, Father,' I said, as I came out slowly. I took my milking gourd to sweeten it, and after I had done this I went out to milk the cattle. My stepmother didn't say anything. She just went on doing her job.

My father said to me, 'Milk your cows, and when you finish go and wash your hair. You look like you slept in the fireplace.'

I finished milking the cattle and went to wash my hair.

So now I knew how my stepmother felt about me. I wasn't happy at all, and I began to think that I should look for my own mother. I also became very different with my stepmother; I tried to be very nice to her. I got up in the morning and swept the house before I went to milk the cattle. I was just working so she would love me like her own children. But she never called me any nice names like the ones my grandma used to call me; she just called her own children by these names. I don't once remember my stepmother sitting down and talking to me. I also don't remember her ever arguing with me. I sometimes think she didn't need to talk to me because she had her own children. But I also sometimes think that people shouldn't hurt little children. If a little child doesn't feel liked and she doesn't have anyone else to go to, she will work extra hard hoping she will be liked. If the person doesn't respond to that effort the little child will never be able to forgive that person in her heart as long as she lives. It still hurts to remember the bad times I had when I was growing up.

In 1958, father married a third wife. She was a Masai girl from a well-off family, very young, beautiful and with good manners. She was not afraid of my father at all and did everything the way she wanted. I kind of liked her. Because she was young she would play with me sometimes. She knew my own mother was gone, but she didn't mind doing things for me. I was amazed when she asked me if I wanted my clothes to be washed. She used to come to help me look after the cattle so I could go to take a bath or play with other children. She wanted me to look good all the time and combed my hair after I had taken a bath. She was like a real mother to me. When I went to a traditional children's dance, she always gave me a compliment. I had a good time with her for a year and a half, but she left and I went back to the same old life.

One day the cattle escaped. They went to a Luyia farm and ate a small amount of corn. I knew that when my father found out I would be punished. I determined that I must run away to look for my mother. My brother saw me when I got home with the cattle and told me to look out because my father knew about the cattle.

'I think they are waiting for you to go in before they punish you.'

'No, no one will punish me,' I told him. 'You just look after the cattle.'

It was about five in the evening and I left right away. I had heard that my mother came from very mountainous country. I could see some mountains from where I was but it never occurred to me that they might not be the right ones. I just started walking slowly in that direction.

I walked until it was almost dark. It must have been about six-thirty because in Kenya on the Equator, it gets dark at the same time all year at around – seven o'clock. I was in the middle of a cornfield. I decided to sleep right there hoping that a wild pig wouldn't come and eat corn at night and find me there. I didn't have anything to eat and I was very frightened. I wanted to stay up and watch over myself but I fell asleep. At one point I woke up and heard the birds singing. I thought it was morning but then realised that it was still night time. At seven at night in Africa it is usually dark but the birds may still be singing as they fly home to their young.

The next morning I made my way towards the bottom of the mountain. It was about 40 miles away, and I reached its base at about six o'clock. Its name was Kapmasai (the place of the Masai). I was weary and couldn't walk any further. All I could see were rocks. There were many deep and narrow ridges and when you looked at the rocks from a certain angle you would see 'mother' rocks carrying their 'children' on their backs.

I went onwards looking for a house to ask if its owner knew my mother. I walked up to a little house in the bush.

'Can anyone tell me if they know a woman named Jerusio?' I said. An old lady came out.

'Who did you say you were asking for, child?' she said.

'I'm asking for my mother. Her name is Jerusio.'

The old lady asked me to come in for a few minutes. She said that she would ask some people in the neighbourhood if they knew anyone with that name. I was so tired that all I wanted to do was just sit somewhere and go to sleep but I was very happy when she said that she would help me to look for my mother.

The old lady made dinner for the evening. She had one son who looked older to me than my father, but he wasn't married. His mother still cooked for him. The lady gave me my food, I ate, and when I was finished I fell asleep right away. The next day she asked me when I had last seen my mother. I told her that it was when I was six or seven, but that I knew that she lived in these mountains, because my father had told me that many times. She asked me which mountains my father had said that my mother lived in. I answered that the mountains were my mother lived were about 100 miles from my home.

The woman finally realised that I was just a runaway child and that I didn't really know where I was going. She didn't know who my parents were either. She began to show more affection to me as though she were my mother. I liked her and called her grandmother. She was really being affectionate towards me because she had decided that she would have me initiated for her son to marry. She went around spreading the word.

The women in the neighbourhood came to see me and they all asked me the name of my father. I told them his last name and his first name. I was beginning to wonder what was going on. I could hear some women when they left the house talking.

'She is too young. She can't be initiated.'

The woman who was going to initiate me turned out to be my aunt Cecilia, my father's sister. She came to see me because the other women had told her that the child she was going to circumcise was too young.

'If her parents try to sue you, you will go to jail,' the other women told her.

I told her how I had arrived there, and she asked me the name of my father. As soon as I told her she knew who he was.

'I must take this child with me,' she told the old lady, 'she is our child.'

She took me to her home with her. I was very glad to be taken by her so that I didn't have to be circumcised. I went and stayed with Aunt Cecilia for a month and a half. She was very upset with my father. She didn't want to tell him that she had found me right away because she thought father shouldn't let me look after cattle alone.

Father had looked for me for two months and had given up hope. He had gone to two soothsayers and they had told him that I was dead. Everyone was very sad in the family. Aunt Cecilia sent someone to tell my father that I had been found. The family was shocked to hear that I was still alive. They had mixed emotions – both sadness and happiness.

Father came to take me home. No one had told me he was coming. I was playing outside with other children when suddenly I saw my father standing there. I tried to run away from him because I thought he was going to punish me. He told me not to run away from him.

'You don't know how happy I am to see you,' he said.

Aunt Cecilia told my father to let her talk to me.

'You'll be all right,' she said. 'Your father is not going to punish you.

He says you're not going to look after the cattle alone any more.'

We left the next morning. When I got home in the evening, all the children came to hug me. They were very happy to see me. I didn't look after the cattle for two weeks. During that time I only looked after the baby and played with the other children. Father never punished me again. My running away had made him gentler towards me. It also made him listen to me, and we spent a lot of time talking together like father and child. At first I couldn't talk to him because I was afraid of him, but later I was able to tell him that I wasn't going to look after the cattle. I would never have dared to say something like that before for fear of being punished.

We had lived in Luyia country for three years. Father now decided that we would move further west to a place called Bungoma which was near Uganda. The country belonged to the Bukusu people. Father went ahead of us to find a suitable place. He found a Nandi family that he and the livestock could stay with for two weeks while he built a house for the rest of the family.

My stepmother was to stay behind with most of the children until my father had built the house. The family was too large to take us all at once. My brother Kipsang and I went with my father because we were the older children, and father would need help on the way. My stepmother ground corn for us for our journey.

It took us almost three days to get there. Each day my father would stop at five o'clock, and we would set up camp. Our job was to look for firewood. When we had gathered enough firewood we would make a fire, and when the fire was ready we would gather round it and drink our milk. My brother and I drank milk that I had milked the morning that we left, and father would drink milk that he had brought with him. That milk was our meal for the night.

'Is milk our only food for today?' my brother asked me.

'Yes,' I said to him.

'Rotten luck,' he said.

You may think that having milk for a meal was something bad but it wasn't. Our real problem was the blanket. We had only one, a small one for a single bed. We didn't have any bed either, so we had to sleep on one half of the blanket and cover ourselves with the little that was left over. We disagreed about the blanket all night long. My brother would give me a sneaky little punch in the ribs, and I would turn around and give him a black eye. Finally Father exploded.

'That's it! I've had enough of your problems.'

We stopped.

During those two days that we camped outside, it seemed to me that my father didn't go to sleep at all. When we fell asleep at eight o'clock, he was standing beside us with his spear and club in his hand and with a sword in its scabbard tied round his waist. We weren't afraid to sleep outside because we thought our father was a hero. We thought that no one would dare to do anything. With him around we were completely safe.

We finally got to our destination. There weren't any boys in the family we were staying with, just girls. It didn't bother my brother that there weren't any boys but what did bother him was the way the children stared at us. When we arrived, they all came and stood around not saying anything at all. Poor flat-chested me! I was slender and tall – the same height as they were. I didn't recognise that they were staring at us because I was too busy staring at them myself. I was saying to myself, 'Look, I'm as tall as they are. Why aren't they flat-chested like me?' We hadn't been introduced yet.

Kipsang took me outside and said: 'Tapsubei, did you see how they stared at us?'

'No,' I said to him, 'I wasn't aware of that.' I then asked him, 'Did you see those two girls?'

'Yes,' he said, 'What about them?'

'Did you see how developed they are, but they are just the same height as me?'

My brother was a little more clever than I was then. He told me not to panic, but to go and ask them how old they were first. He added that maybe they were really women. He laughed silently at his own joke and went in.

But now it was time to gather the cattle and put them inside the fenced enclosure for the night. Father told me to go with the other girls to do this. Of course, the first thing I did was to ask the girls how old they were. One said that she was 13, and the other said that she was 15. Then it was their turn to ask me. I told them I was 11. We also told each other our names. We finished with the cattle and went into the house.

It was mealtime, and I was very hungry. I was looking forward to eating a real meal for a change. We sat down to eat, and my brother came to sit beside me. The inside of the house was dark. African houses don't have any light – people just use the light from the fire to see by. I couldn't see what kind of food there was.

Ordinarily I wouldn't need to see the food because I could just grope in the dark to find the plate and scoop some up with my fingers. But I detected a very strange taste in the food. My brother knew that it was finger millet, but I had never heard of it before. I now became suspicious about my brother; it seemed to me that he was taking two scoops of food for every one of mine. I followed his hand with my hand whenever I took a scoop, and I finally caught his hand shoving the food behind his back. He took a firm grip of my hand and signalled to me not to say anything. As a guest he was obliged to eat the food and he didn't want anyone to know he wasn't eating. I gave him a signal back too, to tell him to leave the food for the other children to eat if he didn't want it.

Then we had to get ready for bed before the fire went out. The people where we were staying just slept on animal skins. You folded them up and put them away in the morning and then put them out again at night when you wanted to go to bed.

The next day father found a suitable site and started work on the house with the help of other people.

A Nandi homestead contains at least three structures, and if there are warriors in the family, there are four. There are always a house, a granary and a cattle corral. There may be a warriors' house as well. The house is a circular building, the walls are plastered with mud, and the roof, supported by a centre-pole, is thatched. There are two entrances, one for people and one for baby animals. There is a wall between the two parts with a door connecting the two. A ceiling is laid across the walls of the house and makes a loft where things are stored. When you pass from the animals' side to the other side there is a depression in the ground which has an enclosure around it on the left. The milk is stored and kept cool here. Traditionally, pieces of animal skin about the size of a platter were used as plates. These were kept in the loft. Small, tightly woven baskets were used to keep food warm, and these were hung on pegs on the wall. Cooking flour was also stored in baskets or in large pots. The cooking utensils consisted traditionally of clay pots, but now people use aluminium ones. Only wooden spoons may be used for cooking. The cattle corral is a circular enclosure made of poles and branches where the cattle are kept for the night and are milked. The warriors' house is like the main house except that it is usually smaller and is not divided down the middle. The granary is a small hut which is raised from the ground on poles so that animals can't get in.

There were ten families in our neighbourhood and we were all Nandi. These were people who had been forced to become squatters on their own land when the British took it from them. They had grown tired of the restrictions placed by the British on the number of cattle they could keep and had left to preserve their freedom. They also preserved their traditions. In fact, as often happens with immigrants, they observed traditional Nandi customs better than those who hadn't lost their land. We lived just like the Nandi of 100 years ago.

There were eight girls in the neighbourhood who were teenagers. Since I was the 'baby' I didn't know very much about what girls should or should not do. There was a lot for me to learn as soon as I got acquainted with the other girls.

It was the custom of my people that all teenage girls should have boyfriends. The boyfriends were always older than the girls because they had to be circumcised. There was no upper age limit at which men had to stop going with girls; they could continue even after they were married providing the girls were not the children of their own generation.

Girls, on the other hand, had a limit on the length of time they could go with men. Their time ended with their circumcision. Once they had been initiated, men would congregate round them wanting to marry them, and, once married, a girl could no longer 'play the field'. So things were different for men and women. It was pretty clever of men to arrange things this way, don't you think?

No one owned a man with my people, and no one owned a girl. A man could not tell another man, 'Don't go out with that girl. She's mine.' A girl would never say, 'Don't go out with that man. He's mine.' No, it was nothing like that. One man could be shared by any number of girls, and similarly one girl could be shared by any number of men. A girl could choose to go out with anyone she wanted.

The customs governing behaviour between boys and girls were very strict. There was no 'hanky-panky'. It was very important for a girl to be a virgin on the day of her initiation. This would bring great honour to her family and would ensure that there would be no complications on her initiation day.

You couldn't trap a man by letting yourself get pregnant in the hope that he would marry you. Even if you happened to get pregnant by the man you loved, he still wouldn't marry you. It was your parents who made the decision as to whom you should marry. Even if you and your boyfriend were so much in love that you decided to get married anyway, regardless of what your parents wanted, you still wouldn't be allowed to keep the baby. It would be given away for adoption because it was illegitimate. If by misfortune it was born when no one was around to take it, it would be left to cry to death after it was born. No one knew about abortion then (in fact they still don't today).

So there was a very high price to pay for 'hanky-panky', which is why no one did it.

Now it was time for me to go to the *sikiroina*, a little house where men and girls meet. The first time I went there I didn't know what to do. I knew that I had to select a boyfriend, but I didn't know any of the men. The men were inside the house making jokes and laughing. When I went in the men were silent for a moment; then everyone started saying, 'Hello, I want my hand to be shaken first!'

The custom was that when the girls went in they had to shake the men's hands. I was so frightened that I began to think it was not a good idea to have come after all. The first thought that came to my mind was, 'Oh my goodness, don't shake their hand, they want to grab you!' But another part of me wanted to act grown-up. I didn't want anyone to know that I didn't know anything. I went to shake hands and we all sat around and talked. All the time I was wondering, 'What is going to happen to me? Should I run from this house?' The other girls were really having a good time. They were joking, touching and hugging the men. I was very shocked and amazed that they let themselves be touched in any way. I didn't know that sitting on their laps and hugging and touching was the pleasure we went there for. I had thought we were just going there to sleep the way I did at home with my brothers and sisters. (At home when we went to bed we just lined up on the floor at one time, nine children and two blankets.)

One of the men tried to touch me, but I wouldn't let him. I slapped his hand and huddled in a corner. He was not so keen really to touch me anyway because I was so young. He was just playing and trying to make me feel at home. But as for me, I was absolutely certain that I wasn't going to let any man touch me at all. When it was time to go to bed we were to tell our leader who we wanted to be with for the night. We lined up outside and the leader asked each of us who we were having for the night. Everyone indicated the man of her preference. When she asked me I told her my father, and everyone burst out laughing. I wondered what had happened. I thought that I was supposed to pick just anyone I wanted. I was lucky that night because the leader, a 16-year-old girl, was very nice. She told the others to stop laughing. Then she called me aside and explained to me that when one came to the *sikiroina* it wasn't possible to have one's father.

'You can't even have your dad for a boyfriend,' she added. After this was finished she gave me a choice.

'You can have so-and-so or you can pick one you would like yourself. If you can't make up your mind, I'll share mine with you.'

My goodness what a relief! I said, 'Yes, I would like to share yours with you.'

We all went back in. The men were waiting for the news. Our leader started telling the men who got whom. The men had no choice in the matter but had to accept whoever wanted them. I was very excited because I was sharing a man with another girl. I was dying to see how we were going to sleep. I watched the leader take her clothes off. I was hoping she would leave some things on, but no, she took everything off. I sat silently for a minute. I was afraid to ask if I should take my clothes off too. I decided to take my top off only and slide inside the blanket.

The man was in the middle. He was facing the other side and was talking to the leader. I lay there so silently that I didn't even move a finger. I was trying very hard to hear what they were talking about so that if he turned to face me I would know what to say. I couldn't hear everything they were saying. I only heard the girl telling him, 'Don't touch my breasts a lot. I don't want them to go flabby.'

I said to myself, 'Oh my goodness. I can't tell him not to touch my breasts when he turns this way, because I don't have any.' I tried to listen to some more, but I couldn't hear anything. I fell asleep while they were still talking.

'Tapsubei, Tapsubei!' It was morning, and someone was waking me up. I didn't answer quickly because I had forgotten where I was. The voice that had woken me said gently, 'Do you know you didn't hug me last night?'

'Yes,' I said.

'Do you know what kind of punishment you get?'

'No.'

'You've got to hug me in the morning before you leave! Hug me quickly so that you won't be late going home. Or you can promise me that you'll hug me the next time when you come.'

The last choice was a good enough excuse for me, and I took it. I told him next time, hoping that I would never be back.

'All right,' he said. 'Go home now, but you must know I'll be waiting.'

CHAPTER FIVE

Growing Up

We were nine children and we always played together. Those who watched us and knew that I didn't have a real brother or sister were surprised by the love we had for each other. I loved playing with them but I had to change because I was growing up.

At night I belonged to the older girls. We arranged a schedule to meet at each girl's house once a week. We met at seven o'clock, and from there we would decide whether to go to our boyfriends or to sleep inside where we were. We worked out an arrangement of going to the warriors' house for four days and then sleeping in our own houses for four days. The warriors were the men who weren't married.

Another custom was for each girl to have a special boyfriend. This boyfriend was the one who would look for decorative ornaments for your initiation day. You would only see him two or three times a month if he was married. If he wasn't married then you might see him a little more often, but not much more. The idea was not to get yourself trapped with any one person. After all, it was only for fun. There were no strings attached unless you let yourself fall in love. Then it would be different because you would both want to see each other more often. You would start meeting in private places so that people wouldn't ask why you were attached to each other.

My girlfriend and I had one friend that we shared. He was a married man, and his wife was a young mother with two children. My girlfriend had him to herself at first but then he became my boyfriend too. She didn't like him very much, not because he was older, but because he was just not her type. I myself liked our boyfriend a lot because he didn't care very much how many times I went to see him. Half the time I went I ended up sleeping with his wife on her bed. When I left in the morning the man would usually have something to say to me.

'I hope my wife will know where to go to look for ornaments for you on the day of your initiation, because she is the one who sleeps with you!'

He was just joking because I was just a little child to him, and he wasn't enthusiastic about having a little child like me kicking him in bed at night.

I was twelve years old when I first went to a dance without my parents. It was not a Western dance, but a traditional dance where girls dance prior to their initiation. It was to be held about 30 miles away, and ten girls and eight warriors from our neighbourhood were going. The transportation was by bicycle with some of the warriors carrying two girls on one bike. We started off at two in the afternoon and got there at seven just when the girls were coming out with their decorations on.

The older women appeared and told us to form the dancing place. For girls who are being initiated this dance is the biggest event of their lives. It signals the end of a girl's childhood, and after she comes out of initiation she will be called and treated like an adult even if she is only 15 years old.

The older women began ululating, and we knew it was time for the girls to start. The bells on their thighs jingled and their whistles shrilled. The warriors' ostrich-feather head-dresses were flowing, and the bells on their legs were jangling. We danced with the girls who were being initiated until midnight. Then the warriors took over and sang and danced for them until two in the morning. Finally we parted. The girls who were to be initiated went with the women for more ceremonies, and the rest of us went with the warriors.

We went to the warriors' house. It was small and couldn't possibly contain 90 warriors with their girls. We had been taken there so that each of us could choose the warrior she wanted to go with for the night. It was so late that every one of us was hoping that she wouldn't have to go through with the choosing business, but the warriors wanted girls, and we had no choice.

Two of the warriors stood out from the rest. They were both skilled cattle-raiders and explorers. They were also both quiet, and didn't say very much most of the time. Kiptaigor was quite a lady-killer because of his good looks. Girls couldn't resist him because of these looks, but the man himself didn't have much to say to girls. He was very business-minded and knew how to talk to other men. In spite of the fact that he was a bit boring, he was popular, and his face and good looks alone knew how to capture the hearts of girls.

Mahindi was the name of the other warrior. Mahindi was a lady-killer and also a ladies' man. He was a man of the world. It seemed like he had a way of understanding each girl he met. He was both poet and lover; he was very delightful to be around, and he had a charming personality. There is a lot to say about Mahindi, but all that I am going to say for now is that Mahindi was fond of girls, and girls were fond of him.

However, the warriors knew that when Mahindi was around it was dangerous for them because all of the girls would want him. They had to be very strict. So that night the warriors asked us to go outside to indicate the men of our preference. For a girl to get to go with Mahindi was close to impossible, but each girl chose to take the gamble. We stood in the traditional line outside, and our leader started from the right. She pointed to the first girl who said, 'Mahindi'. The second said, 'Mahindi'. The third said the same thing, and the fourth, and the fifth, and the sixth. The same choice, Mahindi, continued to be given until the tenth girl was reached. I was number ten in the line, and I was swept away by the voices of the other girls. I didn't understand what it meant to say Mahindi; I was just going along with the other girls.

We went back in to tell the warriors who had got whom. When the leader said that Mahindi had got ten girls, the other warriors asked Mahindi whether the girls could go back outside and choose again.

'You can't possibly have them all, Mahindi!'

Mahindi said that he didn't have any objections.

'You can ask them all to go back outside to make a second choice, but I want to have the young one for myself.'

That was me. He called me to sit beside him to wait for the other girls to finish making their second choices. When the girls had finished, they came in again to announce their choices. Six girls had agreed to remove themselves from the competition for Mahindi on the condition that if Mahindi stayed the next night they would get the first chance to have him.

So that still left Mahindi with three girls from outside plus me making it four. Mahindi took us outside, and if I remember rightly, we didn't have anything to sleep on. Each of us had only a blanket to cover ourselves with. Since we were five we decided to make a bed out of two of the blankets. Mahindi was in the middle, and the girls rotated as long as they were awake. I was nothing special to Mahindi because I was a close relative of his. I had just been carried away by the enthusiasm of the other girls. Mahindi himself thought that perhaps I had chosen him for protection so that I wouldn't have to go with any warrior I didn't like. So Mahindi and I knew that we weren't free like the others to touch, but in our sleeping arrangements Mahindi turned to me and whispered into my ear. He said that what we were doing was all right and that it had been done many times before. Some people had even done worse things. He told me to act normally and not to let any of the other girls know I was his relative. If I did this, they would tell on me so that I wouldn't escape the other warriors next time.

Nothing in his conversation seemed unusual to me except the words 'next time'.

'Didn't you say "next time"?' I asked him.

'Yes,' he said.

'How long are we going to be trapped in this place?'

'Maybe three days,' he replied.

This conversation was taking place at three in the morning, and I was so sleepy I could barely keep my eyes open. I fell asleep in the middle of all the action. The other girls had to roll me out of the way in order to get their turn in the rotation to be next to Mahindi. I slept so well that night that I slept until nine the next morning. At that time I was awakened to have tea. We drank tea and then went to see the girls who were being initiated. The girls would be distributing cigarettes, sweets, soda and tea. We would be singing and dancing for them while they were giving things out and telling their warriors goodbye for the last time. After they were initiated they would be married right away. This was the only time for them to tell their warrior boyfriends goodbye. The style of their lives would never be the same again.

Mahindi was the man of the hour. He was not only popular because girls wanted to touch his body. He was also popular because every girl wished he would marry her. I don't remember a single time when a girl went to be initiated without Mahindi being given mementoes. I think I can still remember some of the mementoes one of the girls gave him this time. The first gift was a pressure-lamp. Next was a suitcase full of things. There was a set of dishes, a lot of sweets, biscuits, a couple of packets of cigarettes, and matches to light the cigarettes. Later he was even given a bicycle by a girl. The reason he was so well-loved by the girls, and by everyone who knew him, was that he was very gentle and had a lot of respect for girls. Any girl who was Mahindi's girlfriend was a virgin on the day of her initiation.

The visiting girls ended their dance the next day at one in the afternoon when the girls went home to be initiated. After a girl had been initiated, the warriors danced for one hour. Then at three o'clock our warriors decided that we must go home. I was so glad to hear the news about going home because I was very worried about that night. I wasn't enthusiastic about another bout of choosing the man of your preference. I was sick and tired of it. We left for home with Mahindi having given many promises to go back there to see the other girls.

Father had hired somebody to look after the cattle so I was free. All that I had to do was to milk the cattle and help my stepmother with a little housework. When I finished I went to bathe in the river. We didn't have any mirrors in our home to look at yourself in after taking a bath and getting dressed. We just used water. After you had taken a bath and dressed, you would take a bowl of water outside, set it on the ground, and look at your face. I don't think I even knew that such a thing as a mirror existed. I simply assumed that everyone in the world used a bowl of water to see their face in.

One day when I was looking at myself in a bowl of water my uncle called me.

'Tapsubei!'

'Yes,' I said.

'Would you come here to see something?'

'Just a minute,' I told him. 'I'm still combing my hair.'

When I had finished I went into the house.

'What did you want me to see?' I said. 'Can you show me now?'

My uncle said that he would, and he went to the place where he kept his mirror. This was a leather bag or knapsack. He pulled the mirror out and handed it to me. He told me to look into it, but not to drop it. I looked into the mirror, and it took me a few minutes to realise that the face in the mirror was mine.

'Do you like it?' he asked me.

'Do I like what?' I replied. 'Are you asking me if I like the person inside this thing?'

'Yes,' he said, 'but do you know that the face inside that glass is you?'

'Is the face inside there really mine?' I can't describe today what I felt then. What I can still remember was that I tried to touch the other side of the mirror to feel if I could find my face on the other side. My uncle told me that the face was always on one side only, the side I was standing on.

I was still not convinced that this was really my face and repeated my question once again. Finally convinced, I couldn't believe how good-looking I was.

'I didn't know I was as beautiful as this,' I told my uncle.

My uncle by this point was laughing so hard that he almost split his sides, but that didn't stop me. I went right on talking to him.

'How I'm looking forward to telling my sisters! I wonder if they see me the way I appear in this mirror. I'm going to tell them how beautiful I am, and if they don't believe me, I'll ask them to come and see me themselves in this mirror!

'I must go home now,' I told my uncle. 'I'll be back in the evening to milk the cows.'

'But you weren't supposed to go today. You were supposed to go tomorrow,' he said to me.

'Yes, I know,' I said. 'I just want to go home for a little bit.'

Inside I was dying to get home to tell everyone how beautiful I was. My uncle knew this, and told me to go, but to return quickly. My goodness, did I run! Home wasn't very far, and in ten minutes I was there. As soon as I got in the house, I asked my sister if she knew that I was beautiful. My sister didn't have much to say, but just replied yes. I told her that I hadn't known until today.

My father and stepmother were laughing their heads off.

'Where did you get this idea of your being good-looking?' my father asked.

I told him that I had got it from looking at myself in the mirror at my uncle's house.

'Did you see your teeth in the mirror too?' my father asked.

I said that I had, and he asked me what they looked like.

'Beautiful!' was my reply. 'Everything about my face was beautiful.'

Father had always been critical of my teeth, and now he was trying to let me know that my teeth were not so good. But I didn't care because I was so sure of myself. I had seen my face in a mirror and liked it. I returned to my uncle's house to milk the cows and wash the dishes after we had eaten.

I enjoyed staying with my uncle and aunt because many things were different in their house. My uncle was an army man. He always liked to eat different kinds of food. The first time I tasted bananas was in his house. We hadn't known about bananas at home because the family I came from was a very rich, conservative and traditional old family in Nandi society. We were descended from a very important dignitary. This man, Kibelio, had been renowned and revered as much as a king, although he had earned his fame by his deeds rather than by inheriting his position. Because of him, our family was greatly respected by other Nandi, especially those Nandi who belonged to our political group, the Kabianga. So we only ate real Nandi food. Father never believed in mixing food. We drank only milk and ate a food called *kimiet* (maize-meal cooked into a stiff porridge). Once in a while we drank yogurt mixed with blood, and sometimes my father would slaughter a cow for us. The meat would be roasted or boiled and eaten just like that. Father called any kind of mixed food 'poor people's food'. He couldn't stand food fried with onions, mixed with potatoes, or anything like that. If you cooked something like that, he would ask you if the food was for human beings or for dogs.

I was with my uncle and his family for one month. When I returned home, I went back to the same routine of going to the warriors' house. I was 13 and I was beginning to like going to their house. The warriors were not treating me like a baby any longer. After three months I fell in love with a man who was visiting from Kitale, about 40 miles away. We agreed together that he would come every two weeks because he had another girlfriend 20 miles from his home. He would see her one weekend and then see me the next.

I imagine that this business of sharing one man must puzzle Western readers. Well, it was easy for us because we had been taught it, and it had been a custom for generations that a girl and a man shouldn't own each other. The custom was even stronger for a girl not to try to own a man. She was encouraged to go with as many men as she could because a woman is only free with my people while she is a girl and before she gets married. The reason a girl is allowed to touch anyone is to learn that all men are the same. It doesn't matter if they are good-looking or not. In fact, one way to show your lover that you love him a lot is to look for a beautiful girl for him to go with. It is the same for him. He could ask you sometimes to go with some of his friends.

I can sit back now and understand that the reason a girl and man could be close to each other in this way was that there was no 'hanky-panky'. When a man asked a girl to go to spend a night with him, the girl always knew what the man really liked about her. She knew the man liked her as a whole person. He liked to touch her body, he liked her smile, he saw something special about her. That made a girl feel sure of herself, feel beautiful, and it made it easy for her to be close to a man physically. The things we talked about in bed were only compliments and praise. If that day was the first day for a man to be with you, he would say all sorts of wonderful things.

'I never expected that the day would come when your body would be close to mine. I have been wanting to touch you since the very first time I met you. Ever since then I've been wanting you. I've had a million dreams about being close with you.'

He will tell you if your looks or your personality are what make him feel the way he does about you. If you feel the same way about him, you tell him. It would be hard to know what to tell him if you don't feel the same way about him. The only thing you can do in that situation is say, 'Goodness, I didn't know you felt that way about me.'

The best thing I can remember about Nandi men and girls is that they never led one another on. They were always honest and frank with each other. A girl would have a special friend who would decorate her on the day of her initiation, but that special friend was under no obligation to marry her if he didn't want to. The girl would have him for a boyfriend while he loved another, and he would always tell her who it was that he wished to marry. The girl would also tell him who she loved and wanted to marry, and sometimes indeed it would happen that both loved each other and wanted to get married.

What happened to me was not quite like that. My special boyfriend loved me and wished to marry me after I had been initiated. I myself loved someone else and there was a third man who loved me alone. The one that I loved was Arap Ng'etich, who came from Kitale. The third one who loved me by himself was Mahindi, the man of the world. Now Mahindi, as you have already learned, was a man that every girl wished to have love her, but for me it was absolutely out of the question to love him because he was a close relative of mine.

Mahindi heard that I was in love with Arap Ng'etich. He came to wait for me one evening outside our house. I was already on my way down the path when I saw somebody. I couldn't see very well and I asked who was there.

'Mahindi.'

'What are you doing here at this time?' I asked him.

'I was waiting for you,' he replied.

'All right,' I said. 'Let's go.'

He asked me to go home with him because he wanted to eat supper. When we got to his home, his mother made dinner for him. While he was eating I talked with his mother. I was happy with them because they were my relatives. My uncle was married to Mahindi's sister, and in our culture that made Mahindi my uncle.

After Mahindi had finished eating we sat for a little to talk. Then in the middle of the conversation, Mahindi suddenly asked his mother a question.

'Mother, have any people who are related like Tapsubei and me ever got married in Nandi society?'

'No,' his mother replied. 'I've never heard of such thing happening. But how could it happen anyway? Tapsubei is like your sister's child. You couldn't get married because you are her uncle.'

Mahindi's mother continued (unfortunately for me). 'Even if Tapsubei wasn't your relative, I don't think you would have any chance of marrying her. She comes from a very rich family, and her parents would want her to marry rich people like themselves.'

That was not the answer Mahindi wanted to hear. I was just sitting there listening to the conversation. I didn't even know why Mahindi was asking this. The only thing I didn't like in their conversation was what the mother said about my family. That was insulting to me.

Finally I asked Mahindi to take me to the warriors' house. We left, and I could tell that Mahindi's feelings had been hurt by the answer his mother had given him. His voice sounded strange to me: of death and unhappiness. Halfway to the warriors' house, Mahindi stopped and took my hand.

'Tapsubei.'

'Yes,' I said.

'Let us not go to the warriors' house tonight. I have a lot to talk to you about, so I will look for another place for us to stay. I'm not asking you to go with me as a boyfriend. I'll explain to you when we get there but I promise you now that you will be free to sleep alone with your clothes on. What I need is only to talk to you, not to touch you.'

I began to wonder what was wrong with him. I had no idea what he wanted from me. I agreed to go with him, and we changed direction and went to the house of a friend of his. What he had told me was the truth. He made the bed, giving me one blanket and taking another for himself. We lay down, and I discovered that I was in for the most difficult night of my life.

Mahindi kept me awake all night long.

'I hear that you are in love with that fellow from Kitale,' he said.

'Yes, I am,' I told him.

'How much do you love him? Are you really in love with him? Do you love him enough to marry him?' he asked.

'Yes, I love him enough to marry him,' I told Mahindi, 'but I can't say who I'm going to marry because my father is the one who is going to give me away. I know I love him, but I just couldn't tell my father that I loved someone and that I wanted to marry him. My father would kill me.'

I was so afraid of my father that I would never have dared to tell him that I loved a man.

Mahindi was relieved to find out that I didn't have anything definite planned with Arap Ng'etich. Before we ended the conversation that night, Mahindi told me that he had been very upset when he heard that I was in love with my new boyfriend. He said that he couldn't stand the idea of someone like me getting mixed up with a miserable man like that.

'I wish I wasn't your relative,' he said. 'Then I would work hard to marry you. It wouldn't matter that your parents objected. That was the reason I asked my mother if relatives like the two of us ever got married.'

'I'm sorry too that we're relatives,' I told him, 'but even though we know we can't get married, I'm very proud to have you as my uncle.'

'No,' he said. 'There must be a way we can get married.'

'No way,' I said. 'You are my uncle and that is that.'

By now it was four o'clock in the morning, and I could hardly keep my eyes open. I couldn't take in much of what he was saying. I wanted to ask him why Arap was not good, but I was too sleepy to ask. I remember telling him that I would like to see him the next day because I couldn't talk any more.

I slept until nine in the morning. When I found out how late it was, I told Mahindi that I couldn't stay to drink tea because I had to get home to milk the cows. I asked him before I went if he would come to see me during the day at home. I still wanted to know what was bad about Arap Ng'etich.

I went home to milk the cattle, but although I did my chores all right, I was not happy. I waited until two o'clock when he finally showed up. He was always welcome at our house. Everybody thought that he was just like a member of the family.

We sat on a little hill overlooking our house. My parents weren't suspicious in any way about what we were doing. I told him the reason I wanted to see him was to ask him why he thought Arap was no good. Mahindi told me that the first problem was that Arap's mother was a witch. The second problem was that he only did what his mother told him to do. Mahindi said that his mother was always telling him when to take a bath. When he went anywhere his mother had to pack food for him to eat on his way. Worst of all was that he never went anywhere without asking his mother.

'I bet that when he comes to see you he has to ask his mother! So what kind of future do you think he has?' Mahindi asked.

He left me with my mouth open wide. The thing which had shocked me most was hearing that his mother was a witch. Everything I had had in my mind to say was gone. If there was ever anything miserable to be in Nandi society, it was a witch. If you are a witch, no one passes by your door. People were afraid of witches like poison, and in former times they used to beat them up and then put them into one place so that they could only bewitch one another.

It had been a long time since I had seen Arap. It was almost time for him to come, but my love for him had died. I didn't want to see him any more. As more days went by, my fear grew stronger. I began to think about what my parents would do to me if they learned that my boyfriend's mother was a witch. I didn't know how to get out of it. Four days later he arrived from 40 miles away just to see me. He brought me a pair of red stockings and some sunglasses. The night I knew he was coming I didn't go to the warriors' house but stayed at home. Father had two wives, and the younger one was easier to talk to. I decided to go to sleep there and ask her opinion.

When I got there she asked me why I wasn't going to the warriors' house. I told her my problem. She laughed and then she gave me some sensible advice.

'I will tell you not to have him for a serious boyfriend, because it would not be good if he ever decided to take you to his home. But if you just meet him here it won't be so bad because he is not a witch himself, just his mother. So go to see him, but make sure he knows you're not in love with him, and make absolutely sure that he never talks you into going to his mother's house.'

I was so glad that I had gone to talk to my stepmother. I went right to the warriors' house. The girls went outside to do their routine of choosing their men for the night. I chose Arap, and we slept. The next morning before he left, he gave me the stockings and the sunglasses. When I got home I showed my stepmother what the boyfriend had given me. She said that it was fine to go ahead and use them.

Mahindi, however, didn't like that at all. He finally came to the conclusion that he had to marry me himself. He couldn't wait any longer. I was only thirteen years old, and marriage to me was a joke. I had boyfriends, and in the course of having fun with them and loving them I wished to marry them, but to me getting married was not something real. It was just something to have fun thinking about. In fact, in my own thoughts I didn't think that marriage was a very good idea. I didn't like the life my stepmother had. Our household was that of a very wealthy man, but all of the wealth belonged to my father; my stepmother had nothing at all. That made me hate marriage. I thought it was just a way of keeping women poor. However, I didn't know what a woman could do except get married.

One evening, Mahindi and I met in our usual place and went to look for a place to sleep. Things were becoming difficult now, and we were hiding from people in everything that we did. That night, before we went to bed I told Mahindi that I didn't want to stay up late because I had to be up at eight o'clock in the morning. He told me that he would make sure to wake me up in time to go. I asked him what I was seeing him that night for. He told me that he had decided to commit a great sin.

'What kind of sin do you want to commit?' I asked him.

'I want to marry you because I can't take the chance of waiting.'

I told Mahindi that there was nothing that he could do. He was my uncle and I couldn't marry him. I also told him that if he thought that there was anything that could be done so that he could marry me, he had to ask my father when I was old enough to be initiated.

Mahindi replied that that was out of the question. He said that I knew that no one would ever tell us that it was all right to get married. I asked him why, if he knew that, was he asking me to marry him.

He just wanted us to break the custom. He said that I was too young now to be anyone's wife, but that there was something we could do so that he could marry me when I was 16. The custom was to run away with the girl and have her initiated away from home. After she was initiated the man would engage her in a formal ceremony and then she would be considered his. He would then take her back to her home to wait until she 'came out' of initiation to marry her. This was very bad for the girl if she was young because she would have to wait three or four years to come out and she would not be allowed outside during the day throughout the whole period. The only thing she was permitted to do was look through a window. The 'window' itself was only a little peephole not much bigger than an eye. I could describe it as a prison except that prison is better because prisoners are allowed outside (at least in Africa) during the day to do gardening. People were not allowed to see the girl during this time, but the girl herself could see people through a mask which was made of animal skins and which covered her from head to foot with only tiny holes for the eyes.

The custom of having a girl initiated and engaged was done so that a man could be sure that the girl would marry him after she came out of initiation. No matter what, it was indeed necessary for the girl to marry the man. There was another option if the man didn't want to put the girl through all that. This was for the couple to go and have an engagement ceremony performed secretly. Then they would not say a thing to anyone until the girl was old enough to be initiated. After being initiated, the girl would tell her parents that she was already engaged. If the parents liked the man they would let him go ahead and marry her. If they didn't then they would break the engagement and marry the girl to the man they themselves had chosen.

These were the options Mahindi had when he asked me to marry him. For myself, I had no options at all because I knew that whichever

I chose my father would kill me. I told Mahindi that I wouldn't run away with him. If he wanted me he would have to wait until I was old enough to be initiated at home. Mahindi didn't agree, but he didn't give up either. He persisted in talking to me for three months. I finally gave in and said yes to him, but only to the second option. I agreed to become engaged to him, but not to be initiated. He agreed to that, but didn't set a date for the engagement.

After that day, Mahindi wouldn't let me out of his sight. Every night he was waiting for me outside our house. He also broke the news to his parents who told him that what he wanted was absolutely out of the question. They couldn't let him marry me. For one thing we were too closely related, and for another thing, my father would kill him. Mahindi's parents begged him not to marry me. They tried to tell him how many girls there were who were dying to marry him, but he wouldn't change his mind. He had decided to go ahead with or without their approval.

A girl named Chebwai Kinegat had just been initiated. She wanted Mahindi to marry her, and she told her parents that she would wait for him no matter how long it took. She waited, and what a scene there was! Mahindi told his parents that she could wait as long as she wanted, but that he had made up his mind about who he wanted and it wasn't her. Mahindi's mother knew that he wasn't going to change his mind. She told her son, 'I'm not going to wait for you to see what you are going to do.'

Mahindi's parents moved away and left him to struggle on his own. Things got bad for him, but he never mentioned anything about what had happened to me. I watched him slow down. Everytime I saw him he looked unhappy. Finally he came to see me.

'Tapsubei, I'm going to have to move because my parents have left. I can't manage by myself,' he said.

He didn't tell me where he was going or when he was coming back. I didn't ask either, and I didn't see him for a month. I was glad, not because I hated him, but because I knew that if he ever came back, I would have to go through with his plan.

I now spent all of my time with my sisters and brothers. We had a little house beside my parents' house, and we had some friends who often came to sleep with us. One night our friends didn't come on time. We waited until eleven o'clock and then we decided to go to sleep. At one o'clock someone knocked on the door. My brother heard and woke me up.

'Tapsubei, someone is knocking at the door.'

I went to the door and I asked who was there. A girl's voice answered.

'It's me.' She was one of our friends.

'What do you want at this hour?' I asked.

'Come outside and I'll tell you,' she said.

I opened the door and went out.

'Didn't you know that there is a dance at the house of one of our friends?' she asked me.

'No,' I said. 'I didn't.'

'Well, there is. We've been dancing for three hours already, and we decided to come to get you too.'

I told her that I didn't think that I should go because it was late and my parents wouldn't want me to be out that late. Our friend said that we wouldn't stay more than an hour, and so I agreed. I told my brother that I was going out, but to be sure not to tell anyone that I had gone. He said that he wouldn't and so my girlfriend and I left.

We met the warriors waiting for us on the path. It was dark and I couldn't tell who was who. We jumped on their bikes and rode. After about 20 minutes I asked what was happening, why was it taking so long. I was getting worried about arriving back home late. I told the man who was carrying me that we had to stop, that I wanted to go back home. He didn't stop. I told him to stop again. He seemed not to hear me. I yelled 'stop' once more and then decided to jump off the bike. I jumped and hurt my knee badly. Everyone stopped when I jumped, and before I got up, Mahindi was there holding my hands and helping me.

When I saw him, I knew that I had been tricked. Mahindi was stealing me. I asked him to take me back home, but he said that we had better get to where we were going first. I knew that I was in trouble, but there was nothing I could do to help myself. The only thing I could hope for was that they weren't going to have me initiated.

We reached our destination at eight the next morning. We were given tea, and when we had finished, Mahindi took me to the forest to stay with him. He was afraid that my father might be coming to look for me. I tried to tell him not to have me initiated, but he wouldn't promise me anything. In the evening I was taken to another house. When we got there, no one reacted to me in any way that suggested that they were going to do anything. They gave us food, but I couldn't eat because I was so upset. They tried to make me eat, but I couldn't.

At eight o'clock at night some girls from that neighbourhood came. Everybody knew that I was going to be initiated except me. At nine o'clock they asked us to go to dance inside a lady's house. I went in with the other girls, but I couldn't dance. I was thinking about what father was going to do to me when I got home. At eleven o'clock the women asked all the girls to leave except for me.

When the others had gone the women told me that my boyfriend had said that I was going to be initiated. I cried right away and told them, 'I'm not going to be initiated. I will accept death but not being initiated.'

They tried to talk to me, but I wouldn't change my mind. At one o'clock they called the men.

'The girl has absolutely refused to be initiated.'

The men came in and tried to convince me.

'Why do you refuse to be initiated? Don't you like your boyfriend?' I said that I didn't like him.

'Then why did you come with him?' they said.

I tried to explain, but no one would listen to me. They told me that I must be initiated.

'Not on your life,' I said. 'It doesn't matter if you return the rain back to the clouds, I won't be initiated.'

The man of the house was a tribal policeman. He went out, changed into his police uniform and got his pistol. He came back in, pointed the pistol at me and said, 'Make up your mind now or I will shoot you.'

'I'm better off dead than alive anyway,' I said. 'If you want to kill me, you just kill me.'

He went back out again for a few minutes and then came in looking very angry. He said only two things to me.

'You had better say yes that you agree to be initiated and engaged to your boyfriend. If you say no you'll be initiated and engaged to someone else.'

Then the man said that he had nothing more to say. He told the women when he left to do their job. I said to myself, 'I wish they had killed me.' The women told me that I didn't have any choice now; it would be easier if I went along with them. They went on with the ceremony, and I was initiated in the morning at six o'clock. Afterwards Mahindi was there right away for the engagement.

I was very weak after the operation and was in a state of shock. I remember hating Mahindi so much when he came. I wanted to say something to him, but I couldn't open my mouth. I still remember that the only word I could sound was 'fool, fool'.

That same day, the news got to my parents. They were told that Tapsubei had been initiated and engaged to Mahindi. Father said that it didn't matter that I had been initiated and engaged to Mahindi, he wouldn't be able to marry me anyway. Mahindi had just wasted his time for nothing. My father said no one would make the decision for him of who would marry his child. He told Mahindi's people to bring me back in two weeks. He said that if Mahindi made me stay there more than two weeks, I should never come back to his house as long as I lived.

When I heard the news I asked to be taken back right away. Poor Mahindi! I sometimes wonder why he went to all the trouble. When he heard I was going and that he would never marry me, he said, 'Are you really going to let yourself be married to someone else?'

'That is my father's choice now,' I told him. 'It's not mine any more.'

He told me that he would not give up thinking I would be his wife until I was 50 years old.

Nandi people have a very complicated culture. Sometimes I wonder why some of our customs were invented, and you may wonder how the custom of stealing girls was invented. The custom evolved especially for handicapped men. Often it was difficult for them to find girls willing to marry them even though the men's families would accept the responsibility of looking after the son and his wife. It was just hard for people to give their daughters to handicapped men. Stealing gave everybody equal rights in marriage, and could occasionally operate to the advantage of a girl if she loved a boy and her family was opposed. The bad thing about stealing was that the custom was not so clear about who should be allowed to steal. I think the reason it went on for so long was that it made it possible for someone to get a girl he would never have got otherwise because of the opposition of the girl's family.

Nandi girls were always guaranteed a husband. Handicapped women were married to an old man, a widower, or to a woman who had never had any children of her own. When a woman doesn't have any children in Nandi culture, she would get married herself around the age of 50 years as a husband to a younger girl. The ceremony was exactly the same as though the girl were being married to a man. The difference was that the old woman was really standing in for the son that she never had.

The girl who has married in this fashion would be made pregnant by a man of the clan of the woman's husband, and the resulting children would carry the name of the husband (of the old woman). The children would call the old woman 'grandmother', but the grandmother would look after the children in the way her son would have. Although the old woman is officially the husband of the girl, she really treats her as her daughter-in-law.

Today the stealing custom has gone, but this custom of female husband is more popular than ever, and a woman can even marry two wives (just as her imaginary son might have).

Nandi people believe strongly that everyone who is born or even ought to have been born has a right to live a full and complete life. This is the ultimate and deep explanation for both the marriage arrangements for handicapped people and for the custom of female husbands. A woman who is mentally handicapped is still entitled to have the joy of bearing children. She will just require extra assistance from her family. Similarly, a mentally handicapped man can still raise children in his name, and only requires extra help from his family. The female custom is nothing more than giving the man who wasn't born (but should have been) the same rights as though he had been born and giving the woman who should have had children, but didn't, children.

Maybe I should emphasise that handicapped people are just people to us. We have no institutions to put them in, no pity for them, and just as much love for them as for anyone else. As children, we fight and play with them just as much as with other children.

CHAPTER SIX
Finding my Mother

I went home. When I arrived, my first cousin, Maritim, and his wife, Bot Tarkwen, told my father that they wanted me to stay with them. Since I was not going to be able to move around, it would be hard for me to stay with my stepmothers. My father agreed for them to have me and I stayed with them for a year.

I turned 14 when I was with them. Bot Tarkwen tried to teach me how to act like a grown-up. Although I was 14 now, I certainly didn't know very much. I remember her telling me my stomach stuck out, and that I should learn to stand straight and dress well. She kept on telling me these things until I was really tired.

'I think I'm pregnant,' I told her. 'That is why my stomach is so big.'

She was shocked. She asked me when it had happened.

'When did what happen?' I asked.

'When did you get pregnant?' she said.

I told her a year and a half ago. She laughed and asked me who the father of the child was.

'I haven't thought yet about who the father will be,' I told her.

She laughed some more and asked me if I knew what being pregnant meant. I told her that of course I knew – it meant to carry a baby in your stomach.

'That's true,' she said. 'But for how long?'

'Only for a year, or two years, or a year and a half,' I replied.

She laughed again when she realised how naive I was. Indeed I was naive, but I had already learned how to deliver a baby by then. When I was twelve, I had been taught how to make a woman sit when she was having a baby and how to cut the umbilical cord and tie it with string. The reason I was taught this was in case my stepmother was in labour and there was no one around who could be trusted. People were afraid of being bewitched at that time. I had been taught all this, but no one had ever told me how the baby got there in the first place. I knew that there was a father because I had one, but I had no idea that he had anything to do with the baby being conceived. When Bot Tarkwen found out that I knew nothing about the facts of life, she decided to teach me.

'Do you know why girls are not supposed to have any 'hanky-panky' with men in the warriors' house?' she asked me.

'Yes,' I said. 'It is bad for the girls, and furthermore they're not the men's wives.'

'No,' she said. 'The reason it is bad is because the girls could get pregnant.' She then told me all about how women get pregnant, and about how old a girl is before she can get pregnant and how old a man is before he can get a woman pregnant. When she finished telling me, I was totally amazed. The only question I could stammer out was if she had done that herself.

'Yes,' she said. 'Even your parents have done it to have you.'

'My goodness,' I said to her when I had recovered. 'I didn't know it was that complicated.'

In the back of my mind, however, I had decided that she didn't know what she was talking about. I asked myself if what she was saying could be true. If it was then the world must be a very dirty place. But I just couldn't believe what she said was the truth. I felt that if she had been doing things like that she had been doing the wrong thing. I said to myself, 'I don't think that other people do it that way.'

I began to feel sorry for her. I also couldn't look at other people in the same way. Whenever I saw a pregnant woman I wanted to ask her if she had got pregnant in that manner. Finally Bot Tarkwen herself got pregnant. She told me when she was four months under way. I asked her if she had done it in the way she had told me.

'Yes, I did,' she said. 'There isn't any other way. This is what all of our ancestors have done.'

I had stayed with them for a year when my father decided that he wanted to move to new land. He said that I had to be taken out of the house before he moved. As an initiate I had been confined to a small house, and dressed in animal skins as I described earlier. I was permitted only to whisper, and during the day I had to walk bent over; I could only stand erect outside in the evening, when no one could see me. A ceremony was arranged so that I could 'come out'. After this ceremony was performed it was time for a girl to get married. For me, however, it was a disaster because my father didn't want the person who had been engaged to me to have me. Nandi custom was that no one could marry a girl who had been engaged to another. The girl was known as the first man's wife. There was no one who wanted to marry me for this reason. Mahindi certainly couldn't marry me. Father didn't even want his name mentioned.

I stayed at home for six months. During this time Mahindi tried everything he could to get me to agree to marry him. I was too afraid. Bot Tarkwen had always been someone who could talk to me. She asked my father one day if I could go to stay with her for a few days. My father agreed, and I went back to stay with them. She started talking.

'You're stuck. No one will marry you now because of what has happened to you. What are you going to do now? You are 15 years old, and you have to start a life of your own.'

'I don't know how I'm going to do that,' I told her. I was now mixed up more than ever before.

'The only thing you can do,' she said to me, 'is to go to Mahindi because no one will ever marry you now that you have been engaged to him.'

My goodness! She had me even more mixed up now. She sent for Mahindi to come and when he arrived she told him, 'You have ruined Tapsubei's life. Now you must do something about it.'

I spent about three weeks with him at his sister-in-law's house. I still didn't want to marry him against my father's will. I knew that I could never face my father if I did. I thought of everything I could but there just was no solution.

Finally I made a decision. I said to myself that I had to run to look for my mother. Everyone was out in the cattle corral one evening when I decided to leave. I hadn't seen my mother for eleven years. I had no memory of what she looked like. I knew what country she lived in, and I knew her first name and her parents' last names. I didn't know the names of any of her other children. I had no money when I left and just hoped that I would find some Nandi at the bus station who would help me to get there.

I walked for ten miles. In those days the country was dangerous. It was late 1963 when Kenya was getting its independence. People were still afraid of Mau Mau, and no one would go any distance at all at night because of this. I started off at four in the afternoon and by eight in the evening had walked ten miles. On the way that night I slept in the house of some Nandi, an old couple. They asked me where I was going but I didn't tell them that I had any problems. I just said that I was going from my uncle's to see my mother. Old people, however, are very astute, and they could see that I wasn't very happy. They told me that I shouldn't travel at night because it was dangerous. The old man, Chemartim, asked what time I wanted to leave in the morning. I said at seven, and he said that he could take me with him because he had to take milk to the creamery at that time.

When we got to the town of Eldoret he asked me if I knew how to get to the bus station. I told him that I didn't, but I was sure that I could find it.

'All right,' he said, 'I'll take you.'

As soon as we got there the buses were getting ready to leave. I heard 'Serem, Serem' being called and I told the old man that that was the bus I wanted. He went with me but before I could get on the bus the conductor asked me for my ticket.

'Ticket please. Where are you going?'

'To Serem,' I said.

'Five shillings please,' he said.

I told him that I had only three shillings. I asked the conductor how far that would take me. He said that it would take me only a little more than half way.

'Do you think it would take me more than one day to walk from there to Serem?' I asked him.

'It depends,' he said, 'what time we get to the place where you get off.'

Chemartim, who had been standing there all this time, reached into his pocket and got out two shillings. He gave them to the conductor.

'Please make sure you get her to Serem safely,' he told him.

I didn't know how to thank him. All I said was 'thank you' and not another word. He waited until the bus pulled out and waved goodbye to me. As the bus moved I cried for shame because I didn't know how I would ever pay Chemartim and his wife back for their kindness.

I didn't know where Serem was, so every time the bus stopped I asked if we had reached Serem. Each time the conductor replied that we hadn't yet. I kept on asking in this way until finally the conductor became annoyed with me.

'Child, don't ask me any more. I will tell you when we get there,' he said. We continued on our way and reached a place called Tindinya, the border of the Nandi and the Luyia peoples. The Nandi on the bus started to get off and finally there were only a few of them left. The people who got on in their place were different. Everyone was carrying a chicken, and the bus became very crowded. You couldn't even turn around without being slapped in the face by a chicken wing. The noise of the people and chickens was deafening. I felt I was lost. I couldn't ask the conductor anything because I had been told not to. I decided that this was the end of my life. My only hope was the driver of the bus. At least he was Nandi.

We finally reached Serem at four o'clock. The conductor came to me and told me to get off. I didn't know where mother lived, and to make matters worse, the people looked different. They didn't look like the people where I came from. It was usually easy to identify a Nandi because the ears would be pierced (like mine), but these people didn't have pierced ears. Finally I found an old man who had pierced ears. It was very difficult for me to understand him because he had a strong accent. Fortunately he could understand me. He didn't know mother because I was asking for her using her first name. No one knew her by that name because Nandi people call parents by the names of their children. My mother was called Mother Kiplel after her son Kiplel. If I had asked the old man using that name he would have known right away. But I couldn't since I had never heard that name before.

The old man could see that I had a hard time understanding him. He asked me to sit and wait a bit. I sat because I had nothing to lose, and in a few minutes he came back with another person. I thought that this person was really a foreigner, but when he said hello I couldn't believe it. He was one of the same people. But he was a teacher and his accent wasn't quite so bad. He asked me who I was, and I told him the whole story. He didn't know my mother by her name either, but when I told him her parents' names, he knew who I meant.

He said that the only woman he knew with that name lived about ten miles away. He knew her because he taught one of her children in his school, a boy with the name Kiplel. I said that I didn't know the names of her other children. He asked me how I was related to the woman, and I said that she was my mother.

He couldn't quite understand that, but he told me that he was going there anyway because he had to teach there the next day.

'I can take you with me to see if she is the woman you are looking for,' he said.

We walked about eight miles, and we reached his home. He told me to go on alone from there because it was only two more miles. I asked him before I left who I should ask when I got there, and he said I could ask anyone I met.

'How am I going to know who is a foreigner and who is a Nandi?' I asked him.

'There are no foreigners all the rest of the way,' he said. 'Everyone is a Nandi from now on.'

When I arrived at the place I explained to a stranger that I was looking for a woman named Jerusio Chepkutbui. He asked me what I wanted from her. I was afraid to say that she was my mother any more because everyone I said that to looked at me as though I was out of my mind. I just told him that I wanted to talk to her. He said all right and went to get her.

He came out with a woman I failed to recognise wearing trousers! I began to panic. I almost told him, 'Please, this woman is not the one I was looking for.' I wondered if the woman with trousers even spoke Nandi. They came up to me. My mother had no idea who I was, but although she didn't know me she was very polite and didn't scare me the way I had thought she would.

I was amazed when she said hello to me. She spoke with exactly the same accent that I spoke. She asked where I came from and said that I sounded like I came from Mosop. I said that I did, and she asked me where in Mosop. She said that she knew a little bit about Mosop because she had grown up there and had moved to where she was now about 13 years ago. I told her where I came from, but she didn't know where it was and had never been there.

'So what has brought you this far away from you home?' she asked. 'Are you visiting someone?'

'No,' I told her, 'I'm looking for my mother and the reason I came here was because my father told me that she lived in Serem. The name I know her by is Jerusio Chepkutbui.'

'Are you Tapsubei Suswa?' she asked me.

'Yes,' I said. 'Do you know my mother?'

My mother put her head down and cried. Then she hugged me and said, 'Yes, I do.'

She left and went to call the other children. She told them, 'Hug her; this is your sister, the one I have been telling you was taken by her father from me when she was still my little baby.'

The children hugged me, but they were too young to understand why my mother was crying. They also weren't impressed to see me. They were disappointed that I was their sister. The way Mother had described me to them didn't match what they saw now. Mother had told them that I was her beautiful princess. She had said that I had small, beautiful eyes, nice posture, was clean and had nice manners. I can still remember what my youngest brother said to my mother that night.

'Mother, this is not the one you told us about. She doesn't look at all the way you described her to us. She is very old-fashioned with pierced ears. She is wearing a dress which looks like it hasn't been washed for years. She is so dusty that I think she has been rolling on the ground. If she were mine I would tell her to go back where she came from.'

Mother told him to stop talking that way. If he couldn't stand seeing me, he could look for a place of his own. He was only seven years old! Nowadays he is very close to me and doesn't like to be reminded of what he said.

The older brother didn't say anything at all. He just stood there and stared at me. We went home. On the way I talked with my mother. She told me that she had recognised me when she first saw me, but that since she had lost hope of seeing me, she didn't want to let herself be disappointed if it wasn't me. She told me that when she saw my eyes she remembered my father, and when she saw me smile she knew it must be me.

My brothers didn't say a word the whole way. I didn't think anything of them myself because to me they didn't seem like they were really my brothers. I felt that I wasn't related to these children of my mother at all. They had their own father there, and of course I couldn't call him father.

While they were disappointed with me, I too was disappointed with their place. However, I had no one to express my feelings to, and everything I felt about what I saw stayed inside me. I was amazed that they had no cattle at all, just chickens running around all over the place. I couldn't imagine how they got by a single day without milk. I had heard about poor people where I had come from, but never like this without even a single cow. In the region where I had lived with my father's family, a very poor person would have a least 20 cattle. My father himself had well over 100 head of cattle.

When we arrived at mother's house, people had already prepared food for that night. The food was to be fish and maize-meal porridge. My mother knew that many children where I came from had never heard of fish before. She asked me if I had ever eaten fish before. I said that I hadn't and she asked me if I thought I could.

'I think I can,' I said. I hadn't seen anything else around, and I didn't want to bother them. As you may remember, however, I had no idea what fish actually were.

The fish were little tiny ones with shining eyes. When I saw them in the bowl it seemed to me that they were watching me and knew I wanted to eat them. I set the bowl down.

'What's the matter?' My mother asked. 'Don't you like them?'

'Nothing is the matter,' I said, 'but are they dead or are they still alive?'

'Of course they are dead. They've been cooking for half an hour,' my mother said.

'What kind of country does she come from where people are so stupid that they don't even know about fish?' my little brother piped up. 'Give them to me if she can't eat them.'

My mother understood my problem because she was once married to my father and knew what kind of family his was. She also knew that Nandi children from Mosop knew no foods other than milk, meat and *kimiet* (porridge). She asked me if I thought I could eat chicken.

I was relieved to find that I didn't need to eat the fish. I had never eaten chicken before, but at least I had seen other people eat it. However, that chicken turned out to be quite a story. It was about eight o'clock when they started chasing the chicken itself. I waited for half an hour before they caught it. Then it took 40 minutes to clean it. And finally three hours before it was cooked. By now it was past midnight. I ate and we all went to sleep immediately.

The next day we spent going through my mother's suitcases and trunks looking for clothing that had become too small for her. She had all kinds of shoes, skirts, blouses and dresses. This was because she had been working for British families as a babysitter. I was still young, and anything I put on looked good on me.

During that time mother learned from me what had happened to make me go and look for her. She told me that I had been ruined, that I had no education, I had no talent, and was still very young. She thought that there was nothing she could do herself for me since I had been initiated. She would have put me in school, but now that was impossible since I was considered as an adult after my initiation. She came to the conclusion that the only thing she could do was to find someone to marry me.

Mother had become a Muslim. In this religion both men and women can marry as many times as they wish. Since by Nandi custom I was already married to Mahindi, my mother knew that no Nandi man would marry me. But she was certain that a Muslim would. So she decided to send me to a little town nearby to be taught how to be a Muslim. I was to be there for three months. After I had been formally converted, she would look for the best husband she could get for me. She wanted to find me a husband that I would 'never have to do housework for or go to the market to shop for without a maid to carry a basket for me'. The husband would have a car with a driver to take me wherever I wanted to go, and I would have everything I wanted in my life. Mother had some people in mind who were rich and who were friends of hers. They were rich all right, but mother hadn't yet learned that I had a mind of my own.

The last thing I wanted was to get married. I was still recuperating from the disaster I had just come through in which I had been badly hurt. My mind was not on men at all. In fact, I was looking for a place to clear my mind from everything connected with men. I couldn't bear having my mother going to look for someone for me. I began to think that my father was better. He was willing to have me stay at home for the rest of my life without getting married. But I was trapped now. I couldn't run back to father's house because the reason I had run here in the first place was that I was afraid of facing him after going with Mahindi for a second time.

So I didn't have any choice. I had to go for three months to be taught to be a Muslim. I went to the little village and stayed with a Muslim family. The sheikh or *mwalimu* would be teaching me how to *swali* or pray. The day of prayer was on Friday. Morning classes consisted of learning how to read the Qur'ān. The first thing I had to be taught was how to dress when I went any distance out of the house. There was a cloth like a bedsheet that was tied around your waist, and then another identical cloth was hung over your head and around your shoulders. You had to dress like that whenever you went to the market or to the mosque. The reason was so that men couldn't see your face. That reason didn't bother me at all because I had no reason to show my face anyway. I wasn't looking for anyone.

I went through all of this not to offend my mother. I remember the first time I was taken to the mosque. When I got there the women were lined up on one side and the men were lined up on the other side. Everybody had to take their shoes off before going in. I was very shocked to see what the women were wearing. They were all dressed up in black silk outfits called *buibuis*. I had never seen a *buibui* before. I asked myself if they were witches or witch doctors (herbalists). I was afraid even to go close to them.

The first thing I noticed after joining this religion was how many things the people believed in. They spent their time worrying about witchcraft, sorcery and evil eyes. A *muganga* is a person who tries to make you well after you have been bewitched and who will take the 'eyes' off you if someone had 'put eyes' (evil, of course) on you. The only person who had any money in that religion was the *muganga*. The rest of the people were just working for him. They were unable to stay for any length of time without seeing the *muganga* because there was always something wrong with them.

If a woman was trying to find a man to marry and not succeeding, she would go to a *muganga*. The whole atmosphere for me was just nerve-wracking. It hit me very badly, and I'm sure that if I had stayed with them long I would either be dead by now or in a mental hospital. The thing that perhaps annoyed me the most was that anytime I wanted to go to the bathroom I had to carry a teapot of water to wash myself after I went to the toilet. No one used toilet paper. The left hand was used for wiping yourself, and the right hand was used for eating. Now I'm left-handed myself, and that meant that I had to be trained to eat with my right hand because if I touched food with my left hand no one would eat it. The idea of using a part of your body as toilet paper didn't appeal to me at all. The people themselves are very nice if you are one of them. A person can stay without a job for years – going from one house to another and claiming to be related to someone in the household when there is no relationship at all.

I struggled with these customs for a month. Finally I told the lady of the house where I was staying that I had to return home.

'Why?' she replied. 'Have we done something wrong to you?'

I told her that Muslim customs were not made for me and that it had been nothing but torture for the whole month. I didn't think I could struggle any more. The religion itself was good according to what the *mwalimu* read from the Qur'ān. The people who practised the religion, however, were hypocrites who had turned their religion into a disaster. In one month I had learned enough to know that I couldn't get on with their customs.

So I went back to my mother's home. I got back at eleven o'clock. I was lucky that Grandmother Chesanga was home alone.

'Are you visiting?' she said.

'No, I'm back for good!' I said.

Grandmother Chesanga had never liked the idea from the beginning. She hadn't liked the way my mother herself was behaving with the Muslims.

'Your mother has been acting crazy ever since she became a Muslim,' she said. 'Sometimes she even refuses to eat the food I have made because I'm not a Muslim.'

I was glad I was not alone in thinking that religion was just a little unusual.

Mother got back at five o'clock from her mill. We said hello to each other.

'What is the matter,' she asked. 'Are you visiting?'

'No,' I replied. 'I have just decided that the religion is not for me. I don't even want to get married anyway.'

Our friendly relationship began to deteriorate. I decided to stay with Grandmother Chesanga. She needed someone like me to help her with housework. My mother was only going to be at home for three weeks before going back to her job in the city of Kisumu. All the children would then be left with their grandmother. So my grandmother was glad I was back to help her.

I stayed with Grandmother Chesanga for three months, but those three months seemed like 100 years to me. Her house had bedbugs that could not be killed by anything. Even if you covered the entire house with boiling water, it had no effect on their numbers.

My happiness would last from ten o'clock in the morning until five o'clock in the afternoon when I started thinking about how the bedbugs would be waiting for me for their meal at night. I would go to sleep in a friend's house, but grandmother liked my company a lot, and so I was stuck with her and her bedbugs.

I was beginning my fourth month with my grandmother when a message arrived saying my father was very sick with a stomach ulcer and that I was needed at home. I remember the date: it was 26 May 1963. What painful news! My mother had told me never to go back to my father. However I felt my father was my real parent because I had grown up under his eye. On the other hand, I didn't want to upset my mother. I decided that I would go while my mother was still away. If I was lucky I would be back before she returned.

I left the next day. Grandmother Chesanga had given me enough money to get me to my father's home. When I got there I discovered that my father had been taken away to Nandi country where his mother was living. I went to Nandi myself to see Father and I was very pleased to find that he was getting better. He told me never to go back to my mother, but I was determined to because I didn't want Grandmother Chesanga to take the responsibility for my having left.

I was beginning to understand what my mother and father felt about each other. I knew that I was going to be in the middle between them. Each one would tell me how bad the other was.

I stayed with relatives. They had a separate house which they let me sleep in. I slept on one side, and the sheep and goats slept on the other side. When one stayed with relatives, they were always happy to have you because you helped them without pay. In my case, I stayed there as long as I did because I didn't have enough money to go back to Serem. The lady of the house had promised me that if I stayed for a month to help cultivate the maize, she would purchase a bus ticket for me to get back. I didn't have any choice but to stay and help them.

One day, when I was still hoeing the maize, an old lady came by. She was looking for wild mushrooms. She was a very happy old lady, and she stood there and looked at me working for some time.

'You look very young,' she told me, 'it looks as though you don't even know how to hoe.'

She was right. I had never worked that hard to get something I wanted in my life.

'Can I show you how to do it?' she asked.

I agreed, and she took the hoe and started hoeing. The way she did it it seemed so easy. She very quickly did more than I had done myself that day. I invited her to have lunch with me. We went in, I cooked and the food was ready in no time at all. We ate, and when we finished, I made tea for the two of us. It seemed to me that she was very hungry.

I didn't have anything else to do after lunch, so my new friend and I went out to sit on the grass and get to know one another better. I didn't know how old my friend really was. When you are 15 or 16, someone who is 60 or even 40 will seem really old to you. Well, my friend Kuyaya seemed to me to be very, very old. Now I'm well known as a lover of old people. I've loved them as long as I can remember, and they have loved me too. I became a very good friend of Kuyaya.

She was a lonely woman who had only one son. The son was married, and his wives didn't like Kuyaya. She came to help me every other day, and we had a great time together. What I love about older people in Africa is that as they get old, they love telling stories about their lives. I'm not a historian, but in my heart I think of myself as one because I have always enjoyed listening to stories. It is more exciting to have someone tell me a story than to have a book and read it for myself. There is always a lot more action in a story that is told than one that is read.

So part of the time I spent with my relatives was happy because of Kuyaya. I spent two weeks with her. The third week she didn't come, and I missed her a lot. I didn't know where she lived and couldn't go to look for her. I only knew where her son lived, but whenever I went there, her daughter-in-law didn't even care enough about her to tell me where she was.

'Don't worry about Kuyaya,' she told me. 'She can be lost for a few days and then, when she has decided to come back, she will show up.'

I didn't bother to look for her any more. I waited, just hoping she would turn up before I left. As the time for my leaving drew near, I sadly gave up hope of seeing Kuyaya before I left. A few days before I was to go, it was a rainy afternoon, and I was inside packing. There was a knock on the door, and I went to open it. Kuyaya was at the door, and she looked terrible. I told her to come in immediately as it was raining hard. I told her to change out of her wet clothes and put on some dry ones of mine. I made tea for her to drink. She told me that she had been ill for a week, but that since she knew I was about to go, she had decided to see me before I went.

She was really too sick to go back, so she had to spend the night with me. The next day, however, she could barely lift her head up. She had had pneumonia, and it must have been very bad. She was able after a bit to go out alone with a little help, but she couldn't do much more.

My relatives told me that I had to send her to her home because she looked like she was going to die. I couldn't do that, however, because for one thing she was too sick, and for another, she was my friend. I knew she didn't have anyone to help at her house. I prayed for her not to die.

On the third day, she couldn't even lift her hand to her mouth, and I began to feed her myself. Everybody told me that she was going to die. I tried to imagine her not dying. What was even more terrifying to me was that she wasn't even a relative. She wasn't even a Nandi. I asked myself what people would think about me if she died with me.

But she was helpless, and her mind was slipping away. She would tell me she wanted some tea, and then when I was making it for her ask me what I was making. This went on for two days.

The next day, the day of her death, something amazing happened. She got up in the morning by herself without my help. She went out and came back in on her own. I thought she was really getting better and that my prayers had been answered. She remained strong all day, but began to talk strangely that afternoon. She asked me to help her to take a bath because she was going home that night. I asked her why she wanted to go at night. Why not go in the afternoon if she was feeling better? She answered that her mother and father had asked her to come at night. I remembered that she had told me when I first met her that her mother and father were dead.

I went to bring her water from the river. I boiled it for her and then washed her. She sang all day long, and I gave her food which she ate by herself. I understood her language, Luyia, pretty well, and I can still remember some of the words of one of the songs she sang. 'Oh me! I will be thrown out the house and buried in the ground. Thistles will grow over me.'

Kuyaya remained better until five o'clock, then she became worse again. I took her in and made a fire for her thinking maybe she was getting cold. She didn't seem to change. At seven-thirty, she asked me to make her tea. I made the tea for her, and she wanted it so quickly that she didn't even give me time to put the milk in it. She got up and said to me, 'Please give it to me quickly.'

I rushed to put the tea in a cup. She couldn't hold it, her hands were shaking. I tried to put it to her mouth, but her lip had a hole in it. She had dropped her lip-plug. I tried to cover the hole with my fingers, but it was too late. She took two swallows and died. She slid down as though she was going to sleep. She closed her eyes. I wondered if she had died. In a few seconds she opened her eyes again, and I began to think that maybe she was just trying to go to sleep. I waited silently for 20 minutes, and then I tried to wake her up. She was long gone, and I knew this time that she was really dead. I didn't want to believe it because I had no idea what I was going to do. I tried to lift her up, but it didn't work.

I went out of the house, closed the door and left to go to call her son. I went half-way and decided to come back. Maybe she wasn't really dead. I returned and tried to wake her up again. She was still the same. I ran for two miles to tell her son.

When I got there, her son was not at home, but his wives were there. I told them that I thought that their mother-in-law was either sick or dead and that they had better come and see. They laughed. I had never seen people who laughed at a person's death before in my life. I thought that maybe they hadn't heard me, so I told them again. They just continued to laugh.

Finally one wife told her co-wife that they should go to see before Kuyaya's son arrived. I went with them, and when we got home they went in and touched her to see for themselves. Kuyaya was long gone. they laughed again, and then they told one another, 'Let us cry before her son arrives and sees us laughing.'

I begged them to carry her to their house so that my relatives wouldn't know that she had died in their house, but they told me that they couldn't carry a dead person from the house she died in according to their customs. The person had to be buried at the door of the house where she had died. So I had no choice but to stay there with them. Those people had the worst customs that I ever encountered. They didn't cry as everyone else did when a relative had died. They cried only after they had decided that they wanted to cry. Then they would go outside and wail. They wailed for the neighbourhood to hear. When the neighbours heard they came to wail too. Within an hour there were about a hundred people wailing. The next day people were still wailing, and eating, dancing and laughing. I didn't see anyone who had tears in their eyes except the son. Everyone else appeared to have just come for the food. They would continue wailing 'on demand' for a month.

I stayed with my relatives for three days after the death of Kuyaya. They were angry with me, but they had to let me go because they knew that I was very sorry for what had happened too. They took me to the bus stop, and I was on my way back to my mother.

When I got back to Serem, my mother was really angry. She thought that it would be better if I had never come back because she didn't want me getting her mixed up with my father again. I was given only one choice: if I wanted to stay with her I would have to promise that I would never go back to my father. I had been given the same choice in my father's house too. The two of them never stopped and thought about me. They never realised that both of them were my parents, that I needed to be with both, and they never gave me a chance to explain that I loved them both equally. They just worried about how much they hated each other and each one wanted me to listen to him or her, but no one wanted to listen to me.

When my mother gave me the choice of staying with her if I promised not to see my father, I had to accept for the time being in order to have a place to stay. Father was a little different. When he told me how bad my mother was, he never insisted I agree with him. Mother, on the other hand, really wanted me to agree with her actively that my father was bad. If I didn't do that, my mother would think I didn't like her. Of course that wasn't true, but she didn't know me well because I hadn't grown up with her. I think that she doesn't really know me to this day. At that time she didn't know that I could not be pushed into something that I didn't like. She also didn't know that I never tell anyone something about them that I don't like. This applies especially to my mother and father.

Father was easier because he knew that if I liked something I would speak up. My father and I agreed on a lot of things together. We only disagreed when it came to the subject of my mother. My father tried very hard to share his wealth with me so that I would settle down and stay in one place. He thought that what was making me go to Mother and then back to him was that I wasn't sure of my future. He didn't know that the reason I couldn't settle in one place was the pain in my heart of seeing two people whom I called my parents with so much hate for each other. What I was doing really in the middle of all this was feeling sorry for myself. My father had twelve children from his other wives, and only me from the woman he was separated from, but he loved me very much in his heart. If he knew that I wanted something he would try to give it to me. But what I wanted was the impossible. I wanted him to love my mother or at least not to say bad things about her. It was the same for her.

I loved my mother, but I felt sorrow for her more than love. She had worked hard all her life to educate her children. She had also remarried, and her new husband, although a good man, was an alcoholic. They were very poor, and their lives together were miserable. They squabbled over money constantly like cats and dogs. If I had been in my mother's shoes, I would have declared the institution of marriage to be a terrible crime!

I couldn't understand why mother even mentioned marriage to me. I couldn't imagine what she saw in it. Her own two marriages had both been disasters. Her second husband sucked her dry. My mother would work, and when she got paid, her husband took her salary and got drunk. Many times I thought that I ought to die so that I wouldn't see what a tragedy my mother's life was, but I had a heart that was solid like a rock. I would say to myself, 'Hey, Tapsubei, don't kill yourself. Try to find some place that you can escape to where you will never have to see them again as long as you live.'

I decided that I would never be married as long as I lived. There was only one thing left for me to do, and that was to be a hobo. I was not a proud person, but I was proud of my own two feet and two hands which helped me to get by from day to day. I took to the road. The work I did was farming, and I did it in return for food and a room for the night. I didn't have any need for transportation: my fuel was my blood and my engine was the heart that I was born with.

Some of the people that I worked for would ask me to carry a heavy gunny sack full of tobacco for 20 miles. I would start at four in the morning and get there about three in the afternoon. I would sell the tobacco and return home, arriving at nine at night. In return for this I would get a place to sleep and food for two days or three days if I was lucky. I didn't have a bed; I just slept on some rags which I carried with me from house to house.

I was amazed by the poverty of some of the people I worked for. They were so poor that my father could have afforded to hire a whole family with children, wife and husband, pay them full wages, give them a house, and feed them for 20 years with no problem. I used to feel sorry sometimes when I ate their food after I worked for them. I would say, 'My goodness! I'm making them poorer by eating their food.' Some of the people I worked for didn't have any food to eat themselves. I would work, and when I finished they would give me dried corn to fry with salt. Water was all there was to drink. That was to serve as food for the whole day.

I was a hobo for a year and I had no thought of what I was going to do in the future. The only thing I knew for sure was that I wasn't going to get married. My mother had tried very hard to get me to go to the city where she worked, Kisumu, to see her and to see if I liked the town. I didn't want to go because I was afraid that she would try again to get me married. My mother sent a messenger to see me one Sunday afternoon. The messenger had been told exactly how to talk to me so that I would believe him.

'Hello,' I said.

'Hello,' he said to me.

I just stood there and looked at him.

'Have you finished your work for the day?' he asked.

'Yes, I have.'

'Is this the house where you work?'

'No,' I replied, 'I go to work from house to house.'

'Why do you do that?' he asked.

I was beginning to think that the conversation was a nuisance. I told him that it was because I was a hobo and that meant going from house to house. The man was trying to be friendly to me, but he realised that I wasn't enjoying the conversation. He finally told me that he had come from my mother.

'Your mother is in bad shape,' he said. 'She has been sick for three weeks, but the bad news is that she has been fired and she needs someone to help her move back home. She sent me to come to ask you if you would be so kind as to go to help her pack her things.'

I was very shocked. I thought my mother must be very sick. I asked the man when she wanted me to come and how to get there. I had never been to Kisumu before.

'Your mother wants you to get there as quickly as possible,' he said. 'If you can be ready by tomorrow, we can leave in the afternoon. Your mother has arranged for me to take you.'

I didn't have anything to wear to the city. My clothes were all rags and in tatters but a friend loaned me a dress.

The next day I was ready by eleven o'clock. I couldn't wait because I was worrying so much about mother. The man arrived at one o'clock and we went to the bus stop. What a sight that was! People think that travelling in a vehicle is something Europeans do, and since they associate perfume and the like with Europeans, they try to make themselves match the style, including the smell, of Europeans. But many times, they had to take chickens with them, the chickens get loose, and the effect is a general disaster. The roads are terrible. They have many potholes, the mud is very bad, and accidents are not infrequent. People realise they are taking their life into their own hands when they travel by bus. So saying goodbye to relatives is a serious matter since everyone has in mind that the ones who are travelling may not come back.

The bus ride took about two and a half hours. Kisumu is about 3,000 feet lower than Nandi country and, when I caught sight of the city, the land spread out in a vast plain below us, in my mind I named Kisumu a 'stretched out carpet'.

CHAPTER SEVEN
Bright City Lights

It was a 20 minute walk to my mother's house from the bus stop but it took us almost two hours. I had never been in a city before; my eyes caught everything in the street and I asked the man about everything I saw. I was fascinated by the petrol station. I watched open-eyed as an attendant pumped petrol into a car. The big buildings, the pavements, the street-lights were all fascinating to me. I remember asking if the pavements was really intended to be walked on; it seemed so clean that I was amazed to see people wearing shoes and walking on it. About halfway to my mother's house we met some people who were on strike. They needed more money as housekeepers. The strike had been going on for a month, and the police were mounting a raid to break it up. Just as we got there, the police exploded some tear-gas canisters and people were running in all directions. The man who was my guide took my hand and told me to close my eyes. I had no idea of course what was happening, and while I was still asking the tear-gas hit my eyes. I remember how painful it was. That experience remains vivid in my mind even today.

Going across the street, I had the feeling that the cars had more freedom of movement than the people. A car would come, and we would have to stop for it. But yet, there were people driving the cars. At noon, there was a tremendous, loud whine from the train station. It sounded like a child crying with no one around to comfort and quiet her. I came to learn that it was the sound of a locomotive letting off its steam as it came to a stop. When I returned home I would call Kisumu 'the land where the train cries like a motherless child'. A loud steam whistle screamed for the whole city at noon as well, and that would send me out to watch people going for lunch. Some were on bicycles, some drove, some ran, but everyone was in a hurry. I called Kisumu 'the city which goes berserk at twelve o'clock'. At three o'clock, everything was quiet. The sun was already in the west, and it hit the surface of Lake Victoria. The water glistened like oiled skin. The glassy surface of the water reflected white in my eyes, like a bowl of fresh, white milk.

Something which I remember impressed me especially was the sight of people carrying fish on their heads to the market. The fish were giant Nile perch, three or four feet long, and I was never sure if they were dead or not. They would lie along the backs of the men, women and children carrying them, and their heads would stare out in the same direction as their bearers.

My mother was very happy to see me. I never saw her really happy, but that day she was at least a little happy. We talked until eleven at night. I didn't ask her that night when we were going to pack. I just waited, thinking she would tell me herself. Of course, my mother hadn't really been fired at all. She had just planned it that way so that I would come right away thinking she was in trouble.

The next day she started work at seven a.m. and worked until eleven o'clock when she came home for lunch. She took me to a friend's house and I met her two granddaughters who were both my age. They said they would show me the city.

They had very beautiful clothes and shoes. When they came out of their dressing-room, I was astonished at how they looked. I didn't have any shoes of my own, and the older girl offered me hers. I put them on and we went shopping first. I had 25 shillings (about £1.25). Eighteen shillings went for a dress, and a pair of shoes were seven shillings.

We toured all around Kisumu and I had a wonderful time. I thought the city was like paradise. It was amazing to see the lights go on all night long. I stayed with Mother for three weeks.

I made another new friend, a British girl called Deborah, who was on vacation from her school. She didn't speak Swahili well, but she spoke it better than I spoke English. I liked her a lot and was proud to have her as a friend. She used to take me to the golf course and tried to teach me how to play, but I was too shy to try to learn in front of white people. We had been taught when we were growing up that white people called Africans fools. At that time, the only people on the golf course were white, and I was afraid to learn in front of them.

One day Deborah told me that she had only three weeks left before going back to her school in Nairobi. She asked me what I was going to do. When I told her I wasn't going to school, she asked me why, and I told her I was too old.

'How can you say you are too old to go to school when you are only 16? Everyone goes to school until they are 25.'

I told her that I had gone to school when I was little, but that my father had stopped me from continuing because he thought it was a waste of money to send girls to school. When they grew up, they would only get married. She asked me why I didn't look for a job in Kisumu. I replied that I didn't know what kind of job I could do since I had never been in a city before.

'Do you think you can babysit?' she asked me.

I told her that I could, and she said that she would try to see if her mother knew anyone who wanted a babysitter.

The next day she came running to my mother's house in bare feet looking for me.

'Tapsubei, I think you have got a job!'

I was so happy I jumped out of bed and hugged her. The job was babysitting for a friend of her mother's called Ann. I asked her when I was going to start. She said that I would start next week and that her mother was going to take me.

When I met Ann I found her very beautiful. She was tall with dark red hair and blue eyes. At first she thought I was too young for the job. She had three children, and the babysitter had to wash all of their clothes, dress them in the morning, play with them when they came home from school, make their beds, iron their clothes and clean their room. She said she wouldn't promise to hire me but would let me try the job for a week and if she liked my work, she would employ me. I told her that I had never ironed clothes before, I had never made a bed before, and that I had never combed the hair of white children before. She said she would teach me.

When the children arrived at noon I was introduced to them – Eric, Linda and Alison. They had lunch with their parents and then I took them out to play. After two days, I knew everything that there was to know. Ann told the children they had to make a decision whether I should go or stay.

'Do you like Tapsubei?' she said, 'or would you rather have another babysitter?'

'No, we like Tapsubei,' the children said.

Ann told me she had decided to give me the job because the children liked me. She asked how much money I was asking for a month's work. I had never worked for money before. I almost told her two shillings, but I decided to let her choose the amount. I told her that she could give me whatever she wanted.

'All right,' she said, 'I will give you 100 shillings a month plus a house to live in. You will also get two kilograms of sugar, two bags of maize-meal, two kilograms of meat and a stick of laundry soap every two weeks. I will get you blankets and sheets for your bed and a light for the house.'

You can imagine how I felt that day; I felt as though I had been lifted from a rubbish bin, put on a queen's throne and had a crown placed on my head. One hundred shillings to me sounded like making a million shillings a month. I worked very hard that month and counted the days to the end of the month to see if I would really be paid that much.

I received my salary and I was delighted. I took the money and put it underneath my bed. I checked that money every 20 minutes to make sure it was still there. In the evening I took it to my mother so she could save it for me. Three weeks later I decided to get the money back because Ann asked me what I had done with it.

'Did you buy anything with it?' she asked.

'No, I saved it,' I said.

'What bank did you put it in?' she asked.

I told her I had given it to my mother to save under her pillow. The woman laughed and told me that wasn't very safe. Someone could easily steal it. She said she would take me to a bank if I wanted to save the money.

I couldn't wait to finish work that day to go to Mother's house to bring my money back. I asked her to give me the money so that I could put it in the bank. She told me that she had used it already to buy things for the other children at home. I was very hurt. She had used the money without even asking me, and it was my very first money. I didn't know what to say to her. The only thing I asked her was whose children she had used the money for. I told her I thought I didn't have any children.

I walked away. I didn't want any more discussion. She had put me back to the beginning again.

I worked until I received my salary for the second month. I asked

Ann if she would take me to the bank to save the money. She showed me how to open a bank account and I had my own bank book from then on. This was very helpful of her but, most of the time, I was very frightened of her. She didn't seem very happy. The only time I ever saw her laugh was in the golf club once. I never saw her laugh with her children. I don't think she liked Africans at all, and she complained frequently about them. If her cook asked her if he should use onions in the dish he was preparing, she would reply, 'What's wrong with Africans? They never do anything without asking!' Her husband was very gentle. Her son Eric was like her and never seemed happy. Linda was very beautiful and liked to laugh a lot. She resembled her father and had blonde hair. Alison was little, about four years old. She liked being cuddled and was nice to carry. I loved the children a lot, and it was fun to be with them. Moreover, I liked the children's English accent, and I was hoping to stay with them long enough to learn English from them. We had a good time when their mother was not at home. We would run to my room (which their mother otherwise wouldn't allow them to do), they would refuse to eat their own lunches and would beg me to let them eat my African food, and they would swear to me that they would never tell their mother. After we ate, they would scrub their mouths very hard to remove all traces of food that their mother might see. 'Can you see any more food?' they would ask me.

After nine months I had saved 800 shillings and I decided I wanted to go to school at night and work during the day. I found a school connected with the Pentecostal Anglican Church of God. It wasn't owned by the Church, but the organisers and teachers were Pentecostals. It was open to everybody. I would work as usual until five o'clock and then go to make myself something to eat. Then from six to eight in the evening I would attend school. I would get back home at nine o'clock.

I continued like that for a month, but it began to be very hard on me. I worked hard during the day, and now I was working equally hard at night. Sometimes when I returned from school I would have homework to do until three in the morning. I didn't know what to do. I liked to get the money every month, but I also liked going to school. I needed school because someday I wanted to get a better job. But if I left the job I had now, I would not be able to be independent of my parents. I decided to leave the school because I needed most to stay away from my parents. My mother had been trying consistently to make me feel guilty – as though there was something that I was supposed to do to make her life better. What she wanted was absolutely impossible. I think that if God himself were her child, he wouldn't have suited her.

I went and told my teacher that I had to leave. I was lucky in that although I was nothing special (in fact a little scatter-brained), they wanted to help me. The teacher asked me why I was leaving, and after I had explained my situation, she asked me if I would be able to come twice a week. I told her I would try. In the meantime the teacher looked for a different job for me that would leave me time for both work and school.

One day after school the teacher asked me to wait for her. I wondered what she wanted and I hoped she wasn't going to talk to me about religion. I had my hands full enough already without the religious stuff. But that was not what she had in mind. She had found out about another job in a nursery. I said I liked the idea but I had been with the English family for a year now, and I felt I knew them well. I asked the teacher what the hours of the job were and how much I would be paid. She said the salary would be 200 shillings a month and the hours would be from eight in the morning to one in the afternoon. I would be provided with a house to live in, but no food. The pay sounded good to me, and the early finishing time excellent. I also liked the idea of working in a nursery; at least I would be free from washing clothes and housework. I told my teacher that I would like to take the job, but that I would give her my final answer the next week.

I began to wonder how to get Ann to fire me. First I thought of telling her that my parents wanted me at home, but I ruled that out because she would see me around Kisumu. I thought I could let her call me three times before I answered her. That would make her angry and she would say, 'If you can't listen to me any more, then you had better leave the job.' But I thought that might take a long time to work. Finally I thought of something that she wouldn't like at all; being asked for more money. The next morning I felt very sick inside me and didn't know how to broach the subject. I decided not to ask her, but to ask her husband. I waited until he was about to leave and said I would like to speak to him.

'All right,' he said, 'but make it quick. What would you like to talk about?'

I told him I wanted to talk about my salary.

'I think it is too little, and I would like a raise,' I said.

He touched his head.

'Tapsubei, that is no problem. How much would you like, 250 or 300?'

'Two hundred and fifty,' I told him.

'All right, Tapsubei, I will raise your salary,' he said, 'but you know I will have to ask my wife.' When she found out she was very angry that I hadn't come to ask her. In the morning the husband came into the room.

'I'm sorry, Tapsubei, but you will have to ask my wife about increasing your salary.'

I felt sorry for him because he had run into a problem which was not of his doing. I didn't wait for Ann to cool off, but went right in while she was still angry enough to fire me.

I have never seen people as calm as the British when it comes to making a decision. She asked what I would like her to do for me, and I told her that I wanted my salary raised. She said that she was sorry but she couldn't do that because she was the one who had taught me the job. She said that the only thing she could do was to give me three weeks' notice to look for another job.

'Suppose I find a job before three weeks are up and need to start it. Can I go?' I asked.

'In that case you will have to tell me a week ahead,' she said.

I waited for three days and then told her that I had found another job. She asked me to wait for four days while she got another babysitter. I did this, and then moved on to the new job.

I now had a room-mate, Eleanor. She was a high-school student who had been born in Kisumu. She was a very nice girl, but she didn't know any other life except city life. I started my new job and changed the time I went to school to two o'clock instead of six so I had the evening free. Eleanor was of my tribe, and that made living together easy. There were some ways in which she was different from me, however. She had a boyfriend she went out with every weekend. They would drink until two in the morning, and when she came home the house would smell as though it had been washed with beer. That bothered me a lot because I had never drunk beer before. Those days were also the days when I was still innocent, and I didn't want to have anything to do with men. I was afraid of getting myself trapped into something that I wouldn't be able to get out of. That didn't mean that I didn't like men. In fact some men were good friends of mine – as long as they stayed a distance from me. I was afraid that if I got involved with anyone, it might interrupt the plans I had begun now to make for the future.

Eleanor's boyfriend was a driver who worked for the survey branch of the government. His boss at the time was a young Swede who spoke no Swahili. One evening the two of them came to the house when I was on my own. I was amazed to see the Swedish man there; I didn't believe that a European would enter an African house. The house was so tiny that we didn't even have a chair. We cooked in the same place, slept in the same place, and used the bed for a chair. I didn't ask the men to sit down.

'Aren't you going to ask us to sit down?' I was asked.

'We don't have any chairs,' I replied.

'What do you want us to sit on?'

'We sit on the bed,' I said.

'Is it all right if we sit on the bed too?'

'Of course,' I answered.

They waited a few minutes, and Eleanor came. They decided to go out to eat. My room-mate asked me to go with them.

'No thank you, I have a lot of homework to do,' I said.

They left but in a few minutes Eleanor came back. She asked me to come for only half an hour.

'Let us go and have fun now,' she said. 'Maybe one day we won't be so lucky.'

I finally agreed. We were taken to the finest hotel in the city, the Kisumu Hotel, which was owned by the British in those days. When we got there the door was opened for us. Eleanor knew all about this sort of thing and went in first. I stood back to let the men go in because that is what we are accustomed to do.

Since the European, Kenny, didn't speak Swahili, he motioned me to go in with his hand. I was astonished when I got inside. The entire floor was covered with a rich red carpet. The tables were equally amazing. A waiter took us to a table. It is very hard for me to give you a description of my feelings at the time. All I can say is that it felt like I was going through some kind of ceremony. When we had been seated, we were given menus. The waiter asked first if we wanted anything from the bar. For myself, my mind was not on the menu nor on what the waiter was talking about. I was very impressed by the fancy decorations on the table. The serviettes were rolled into little cones and stuck into glasses. The silverware was incredible. When I turned to my right I could see a dozen or more pieces at my place. On my left it looked the same. I had used silverware before, but never two dozen pieces. I had only used a fork, knife and spoon.

The others had ordered their drinks from the bar. Eleanor had ordered a beer for me, although she knew I didn't drink.

'Here is your drink, Tapsubei,' she said to me.

'But you know I don't drink beer,' I told her.

She asked me to go the ladies' room. When we got there she said, 'You don't have to drink your drink. Just put it in a glass and sip it little by little. You don't have to finish it. I'll finish it for you.'

I asked her what all the silverware was for and the serviettes rolled up inside the glasses. She said she didn't have much experience of using it herself. The only thing she knew was that it was for eating with. What she knew about for sure were the serviettes. When the food arrived you were supposed to take the serviette and put it around your neck. She said if there was anything else I didn't understand, I should wait and see how other people used it.

We went back to the table, and the men poured the drinks. I took a sip of my beer. My goodness! I couldn't help myself but spit it back into the glass. It should have been embarrassing, but the others turned it into a laughing matter. I joined in the laughter too. Kenny asked his friend why I had done this, and he was told that I had never tasted beer before.

I was sitting beside him even though he didn't know any Swahili. He had learned by just watching me that I didn't know a lot. When the food arrived, I tried my best to eat with as many pieces of silverware as I could. Watching me eat, the man could see that I was having a lot of trouble. He told his friend to suggest I eat with the fork only.

When we had finished we moved from the dining-room to the bar. Being in a bar was to me synonymous with being of very low quality.

The only black girls were the two of us, and to make the matter worse we were with two men. My room-mate and her boyfriend were happily drinking like fish. That left Kenny and me looking as though we were a boyfriend and girlfriend at the end of breaking up. We had nothing to say to each other apart from the language problem. I could see that he liked me from the way he was trying so hard to communicate. When we finally went home Kenny got out of the car and asked the other man how to say 'I hope that I will see you again' in Swahili.

I thought of him for two days, wondering what I would do if he liked me. I kind of liked him too. The only hope I had was that he wouldn't like me.

After I had worked in the nursery for four months, I discovered that I didn't like all children equally. I was very disappointed and ashamed of myself. It didn't feel right to hate little people of only three or four years. The children came from all kinds of different backgrounds, and with only one exception I was unfamiliar with these backgrounds. The only children I knew anything about were the British children because I had babysat for them for a year. I was too young to know how to deal with all kinds of children.

Three weeks after I had met Kenny I had forgotten him. Then one day he turned up on his own. He had learned a little Swahili and he asked me something like this: 'Me you go eat.' I spent more time teaching him Swahili than going out with him. I taught funny things rather than real language. It never occurred to me that he would use it with other people. I remember one day I was nervous when an old lady came to my house and he was in. I thought he was going to try the Swahili I had been teaching him on her because he was so friendly that he talked to everyone.

I remember the first thing I taught him. When he asked me how to say 'Hello' in Swahili, I told him to say 'My golly gosh, this child is so beautiful'. And when he was meeting her for the second time, I told him to say 'My heart hasn't stopped beating fast since I first saw you'. Then I taught him to say 'I think if we were to be locked in a room for ever together, I would never be tired of being with you'. The thing that was fun about this was that I didn't know the language (very well) myself. I used to go to collect Swahili from friends so that when he came on Saturday I would be ready to teach him. After he had learned Swahili fairly well, he told me that he had known all along because whenever I taught him something new he would go and ask his driver what it meant. I was very disappointed because all this time it had been so much fun for me.

Kenny knew he was only going to be in Kenya for two years. I liked him, but I didn't want to be disappointed when he left. I kept my friendship at a distance from him. He felt strongly about our friendship, but he could see that it would be very hard for me to accept going to any other country. It was sad for both of us because he had no way to stay in Kenya. Our friendship became painful. One side of me still didn't want to get married, but another side of me liked him very much. He had the same problem. Part of him wanted to remain in Kenya to be with me and yet his contract was finished in eight months. He knew that the Kenyan government wouldn't give him any more time, especially if he were to say that the reason for his wanting to stay was an African girl.

I finally decided to make it easier for both of us. I was fed up with the job. I was up to my ears in children in the nursery. There were over 100 of them and just two teachers, or rather one and a half since the other teacher always had a backache and didn't do much.

The ages of the children were from two and a half to four years. Some of them didn't even know to tell you when they had to go to the toilet. They just messed themselves and came crying saying, 'Look, look'. I would clean up to five children a day. I decided to give up the job and I wrote to Kenny saying I was sorry but that I couldn't wait any longer to see him. I said goodbye and I hoped that we would meet again.

'We know the mountains can't meet, but human beings can meet again,' I told him. I left the note with Eleanor.

That afternoon I bought a radio to listen to when I was back on the farm, and I went to the school to tell them I wouldn't be coming any more since I had left my job. The head of the school liked me a lot and wanted to help me. She said she would look for a place for me to stay in the Christian Centre. I told her that I had made up my mind to go home to my father, but that if she was willing to help me I would just go for a few months to see my family. When I came back I would see if she had a place for me. I was glad that I had someone to help me, and I knew that I would see her when I returned to Kisumu. We said goodbye, and I went home to pack my things.

I didn't have much to pack: two glasses, two bowls, two plates, two pots, one blanket and one bedsheet. I put them all in my suitcase. I hadn't seen my family for a year and a half and I was looking forward to showing them that I could make it on my own.

I got home at three in the afternoon. My brother Kipsang, the next oldest after me, saw me first. All the other children were still there; I was the only one who had left. When my brother saw me, he called all the children.

'Everybody come out! I see Tapsubei coming!'

They all ran to embrace me and welcome me with warmth. In all, 14 children were embracing me. Some of them were hugging my legs, some my hands, and some just touching me. My two stepmothers Korge and Bot Agni joined them. My father was standing aside watching his children running to their sister. After the children had finished hugging me, my father came to shake hands with me. I stayed at home for two wonderful months. My sisters had grown up, and they completely spoiled me by not letting me do any work at all. They all loved me like my father. Although we were all old enough to know that we weren't really from the same mother, nothing had changed, and we were just the way we had always been.

While I was there my sisters wanted to know about city life, but I didn't want to tell them anything good about it. I remembered what I had gone through to get there and it was not pleasant. I tried as much as I could to tell them how bad the city was. There were in the family at this time about 30 people, including the parents. We had three divisions or groups. The parents in one group, the boys in another, and the girls in a third. Bot Agni was exceptional. She was very easy to be with. She was a sloppy person who didn't care what her house looked like, but the best thing about her was that she never told anyone what we girls talked about.

Since I was still thinking about Kenny, I decided to ask my sisters their opinion, but I didn't let them think I was asking for myself. I told them that I was just asking them as a question. For example, suppose one of you met a European, and he told you that he wanted to marry you. What would you do?

One of my sisters said that she wouldn't even go close enough to a European for him to say he wanted to marry her. Another one said that she couldn't imagine even touching one. Others said that if they heard that some Europeans were coming, they would lock their doors and not come out until they had left. My last sister told me that if a European man came and asked for her even that night, she would say yes to him and let him take her right away.

'Anyone can take me away from this madhouse,' she said. 'Then I won't have to get up in the morning and go to milk the cattle. I won't have to look after the cattle. I will be taken everywhere by car. I will sleep in the morning until nine o'clock. Then I will get up, take a bath, make tea and drink it, and go back to bed!'

Her answer made everyone in the house laugh because we hadn't known how much she hated farm life. My stepmother Bot Agni's answer was that if a daughter of hers ever wanted to marry a European, she would do everything she could to persuade her not to marry him. She had heard that if a European married an African girl, he would take her to his country. They would live together until the man decided that he didn't want her any more and then he would put the poor girl in a freezer to be frozen to death.

My question was thus answered in less than an hour. The answers were all different, and not a single one of my sister's answers was any help. The only thing that helped me forget Kenny was what my stepmother had said.

When two months were up, I told my parents that I had to go back to my job. I didn't tell them that I didn't have one because if I had said this, my father wouldn't have allowed me to go back.

I left the next morning. On the way I decided to go to visit Grandmother Chesanga – that is, my mother's mother. When I got there she was outside picking vegetables and didn't see me.

'Hello, Grandma, I'm here,' I said.

Grandmother Chesanga had a strange way of saying hello.

'Oh, who is it?' she asked.

'Me, Tapsubei,' I said.

'Oh, poor you. Why did you come to this miserable house? We are starving to death here. I hope you had something to eat before you came. Otherwise you may starve to death with us tonight.'

While she was telling me all of this, she hadn't even said hello to me.

'All right, Grandmother, I'll be leaving then because I wouldn't want to starve to death with you,' I told her.

'No, don't just go like that,' she said. 'We haven't even said hello to each other. I don't think that we'll starve tonight because I had just picked some vegetables when you arrived.'

'Make up your mind, Grandmother, do I go or do I stay?' I asked.

'Oh, stay for a few days, and we'll try to survive through them,' she replied.

I had bought a few things for her on my way to visit her. She didn't drink tea, so I had brought her a blanket, some meat and some oil. I knew that those were things that she liked. My grandmother, however, never said that she liked the things you brought for her. Instead she said, 'Oh, why did you bring all of those things?' Even though she was happy in her heart, she scolded you for bringing things to her.

When she pretended to do this, I would go along with her.

'Oh, I'm sorry, Grandmother, I didn't know that you didn't want anything. I'll just take them back with me tomorrow morning,' I said.

When my grandmother heard that she was prepared.

'Oh, why bother taking them back? I'll just keep them here,' she said.

The only person my grandma would stay with and laugh with was me. One reason was that I had understood what kind of a character she was. Another reason was that I never stayed with her for more than a month. That made it easy for us to laugh a lot when we were together. My other relatives, who had been living all of their lives with her, were fed up with her behaviour. No one thought it was funny any more. For me, however, she was so funny that always looked forward to seeing her. This time I stayed with her for two weeks. Every morning I would turn the radio on. She made sure everybody kept quiet while I was listening. When I had finished she would ask me what I had heard.

'I was listening to the news,' I told her.

'What kind of news was it?' she asked.

'News from all over the world,' I said.

'How did it get there?'

'It got here by travelling through the air.'

The idea that the news got to the radio by travelling through the air sounded strange to my grandmother.

'I've never heard of anything like that,' she said, 'and I thought I was grown-up. From now on I won't be able to think I am grown-up because there is lot that I don't know. Isn't it amazing that some words can just come and pass right by where I am standing and go inside that thing?'

Grandma always went to meet her friends to drink Nandi beer in the afternoons. When she came home in the evening she was drunk. She had a sister she had never got along with, and whenever they met at a beer-place, they argued. One evening when she came home my grandma asked me to turn the radio on.

'Everybody be quiet for a few minutes,' she said.

'Shut it off now,' she said after a few minutes.

When I had turned the radio off, she questioned me.

'Did you hear that?' she said. 'Did you hear how she started in on me? I didn't say a word to her at all. I'm glad that the radio was there. It will help me to tell the truth because no one ever believes my side of the story. Now the truth will come out, thanks to the radio. I've told my sister that will be the end of her insults.'

I was shocked that she thought the radio would just pick up any conversation from the air. It was hard for me to explain to her how the radio worked. She was very upset because she hoped the radio would help her to tell people the truth about her sister.

In the morning I tried to explain to her again how the news got into the radio. I thought she had understood, but in the evening she asked me again if I had heard on the radio what had happened to her that day.

'If you haven't heard, you turn that thing on. I bet you'll really like this one. It was a mess.'

I was tired, and in the end I had to tell her that the radio didn't understand Nandi.

CHAPTER EIGHT
Missionaries and Shopkeepers

Two weeks later I returned to Kisumu and went straight to the Christian Centre to see my teacher. She asked me if I was looking for a job, I said I was and she told me my old job at the nursery was still open.

'I don't want to go back to that job even if I am paid 1,000 shillings a month.' I said. 'If you don't mind, I would like to stay here at the Centre for a few weeks while I look for another job. I have a little money, enough to stay for a month.'

My teacher said that she wouldn't mind if I stayed.

'It's too bad you're not a Pentecostal,' she said, 'because there is a job in the Pentecostal Church. They need a Christian girl to work with a newly arrived missionary couple from Finland, who speak a little Swahili.'

I was prepared for any kind of job when I returned to Kisumu but I wasn't prepared for religion.

'Can anyone join this religion?' I asked.

'Yes, God needs all kinds of people,' she said.

I knew that I really didn't need the religion, only the job. My own family had become Catholic when we moved back to Nandi country, and I had become one too but I had dropped out because of the kneeling. I'm sure a lot of people didn't understand the language spoken in church but they didn't seem to have any problems kneeling without understanding. I asked my teacher what people did in church.

'Well, why don't you come with me on Sunday and see for yourself?'

I got up on Sunday and put on my best clothes and some jewellery as well. When we met she had something to say to me.

'In our church we don't believe in wearing jewellery or putting on nail polish,' she said.

'Why?' I asked.

'We believe that God didn't make people with all of those things. We know that wearing such things is the work of Satan,' she said.

I almost asked her about clothing, but I decided some questions were better left unasked.

I had found one thing wrong about their beliefs already, before I even got to their church. I wondered why these people thought that wearing jewellery and fingernail polish was the work of Satan. I thought that wearing clothes should then also be a work of Satan. Although I hadn't read the Bible, I was sure that God hadn't made man with clothes on because I had seen children being born nude. Nevertheless I took off my jewellery, put it away and we left.

When we got there the teacher introduced me saying, 'This is our new sister.'

'God be praised,' the others replied. We went into the church, and the service was opened with a little prayer.

'Let us sit down and close our eyes to pray before we start our gospel for today.'

I thought to myself, thank goodness they didn't say 'Let us kneel to pray'. We all sat down, and the pastor started praying for the people. In the middle of the praying I heard a voice from the front row. It was an unpleasant sound that was inbetween a cry, a moan and speech. It couldn't be understood. I wondered what was happening, and while I was wondering, the number of voices increased. I decided to stand on a chair to see what was happening. I saw some women who looked like they were having an epileptic fit. I wondered what had happened to cause all of them to have seizures just now at one time in the church. I completely forgot I was standing on a chair until a lady next to me asked me to sit down. We finished at one o'clock, and my teacher took me back home.

As soon as we got in the car, I asked her if she had any idea what had happened to the women in the front of the church.

'Which women?' she asked.

'The ones who were crying,' I said.

'They weren't crying,' she said. 'They were the people who have received a special gift. They speak in tongues.'

She told me that the disciples of Jesus used to speak to all the different peoples in the world in that language so that they would know that God loved them all. I asked her if the language was given to Jesus's disciples to speak to all peoples, then wouldn't these women who were speaking be understood by the other people in the church? She said no, that speaking in tongues doesn't happen in only one language. It can happen in Russian, Arabic, Hebrew or Greek. I wanted to ask why somebody in Africa would speak in Hebrew or Greek if no one in the church was Greek or Jewish. I decided not to because in Nandi culture we were taught that if you go to another country where people have a different way of feeling things, you shouldn't question their feelings. Just leave them the way they are as long as you know who you are yourself.

I didn't ask my teacher any more, but I was bitten with curiosity. I decided that I must join this religion, not only for the job. I also wanted to experience speaking in tongues myself.

I worked with my new employers for a year and during that time went to church regularly and took classes preparing to be baptized. We were asked to choose Christian names; I chose Jane and it has been my name ever since. I prayed hard that I would speak in tongues. I was sure I had a chance because during the entire time I was there, the only people who spoke in tongues were women.

The day of my baptism I invited my cousin, Karen, to come and watch the ceremony. After the ceremony the people started praying and, as usual, the women started promptly to speak in tongues. Afterwards, I asked Karen what she had thought of the church service. She said that she didn't have a chance to think about the church at all because she was so shocked by the crying of the women speaking in tongues.

I tried to explain to her about speaking in tongues as I understood it. She asked me if men also spoke in tongues and I told her that I had never heard one do so. She asked me if I had ever wondered why only women spoke in tongues.

'No, what are you driving at?' I asked.

'Tapsubei, I'm trying to tell you to open your eyes and see the world the way it really is,' she said. 'I'm not telling you not to be a Christian; I'm only trying to tell you not to get mixed up with crazy people. I don't think those women are speaking in tongues under the influence of God or anyone else. They just cry when they come to church because of their problems at home with their husbands!'

It was so nice talking to Karen. After three years of talking mainly with people of other tribes, I rarely felt that I was talking to a real person. Although I understood what she meant, I was still curious to speak in tongues myself. I tried for a year, but it never happened to me.

Nevertheless, I was chosen to go out to witness to people, to be a missionary myself. There was a lot of travelling involved, and I was always worn out by the evening. Also, the country we travelled in was full of mosquitoes, which I had never experienced before. We were divided into three groups: the people of the area themselves, four Finnish missionaries, and me.

We would all go together to some place to witness. We would go to the main market and start reading from the Bible, using things like Matthew 15, verse 13, saying 'Every plant which my Father in heaven did not plant will be pulled up'; or Matthew 10, verses 5–15 where the twelve Apostles are sent out to preach by Jesus and told that 'If some home or town will not welcome you or listen to you, then leave that place and shake the dust off your feet. I assure you that on the Judgement Day God will show more mercy to the people of Sodom and Gomorrah than to the people of that town.' In short, we tried to frighten people into the church. In order to get us to witness, the missionaries used the story of Jonah (who refused to preach to the people of Nineveh). That got everyone working hard, since everyone wanted to do better than Jonah. The missionaries tried to choose good-looking people to witness. At first there would just be the group of us witnesses, but then other people would be attracted one by one until a group of 30 to 40 had gathered round. When the preaching was over, people would ask about how to come to God. We would hold hands and pray for the newcomers. The missionaries themselves didn't say anything, but just stood aside and listened until the time came to pray. Then they would ask people if they had anything they wanted to be prayed for. They told people that Jesus could do anything (open your eyes if you are blind, make you walk if you are crippled), and asked people with problems to come forward.

In the evening the missionaries would leave to look for a place for themselves to sleep and I would be left with the other Africans. Some of the places we went to weren't too bad, but I remember one, Kendu Bay, that was just awful. The mosquitoes were like a horde of locusts.

The missionaries had gone to Kisii, a big city nearby with nice hotels and no mosquitoes, to sleep there. The lady of the house where we were staying had a mosquito net which she used for herself and her two children but I knew I couldn't possibly ask her to let me sleep with them. My feet were burning from the bites as though I had stuck them into boiling water. I reflected on what God had told us to do – to go out among the poor and unfortunate and preach to them. The people living here were certainly among the most unfortunate ones in the world, but I was sure that God had never intended that some of his disciples sleep in luxury hotels while others suffered from mosquitoes! There cannot have been any mosquitoes in the Holy Land when Jesus gave instructions to his disciples, I decided, or else he would have given instructions for dealing with them too.

Before we left Kendu Bay I asked the missionaries if there were mosquitoes at Kisii also. I was no longer afraid to say what I thought. Although we had been taught that Christians shouldn't complain in any situation, I had already decided that if they wanted to throw me out of their church that was their problem. If I was to go to Kisii, I would go only on the condition that I wasn't to sleep in a house without a mosquito net.

The missionaries didn't answer me right away, but talked to each other in their own language for a few minutes. Then they told me that they thought that Kisii only had a few mosquitoes, not a lot like Kendu Bay. Then one of them told me that there was nothing they could do about the mosquitoes really. I replied that I wasn't asking them to do anything; I just wanted to know if mosquitoes were there so I could look for a bus home.

We set off for Kisii and arrived at four in the afternoon. We had an hour of witnessing, and then we visited with families until six. In the evening the missionaries asked me if I had enough money to sleep in a hotel. They thought I would feel guilty because I would be leaving the other people to sleep with families. But I didn't; I was delighted to be able to sleep in peace alone.

Several days later we went back to Kisumu. I was very glad to be back, but the trip had been a good learning experience for me. If I hadn't gone on this trip I wouldn't have known how people in other parts of my own country lived.

What bothered me all the time, however, were the missionaries. The missionaries treated all Africans like sheep. They didn't think that Africans were real people. I sometimes wondered why they went there in the first place. They didn't know one African from another, and they had no respect for African customs. If you told them about your customs and how they were different from those of other tribes, they always understood you in the wrong way. They thought you were telling them that your customs were better than those of other Africans. That wasn't true, but even if it were, it should have been respected as the legitimate pride of a person in his own society.

My time with the missionaries led me to think that they must have come to Africa with only one thing in mind: coming to help those 'poor primitive people'. But when they got there they didn't bother to learn anything about the people they were supposed to be helping and about how they were different from one another. I think that if they had bothered to do this, they wouldn't have tried to drive them like sheep, but would have understood them as people.

It also amazed me that they never stopped to think whether Africans had anything of interest to teach them about beliefs and about life. The only things they would talk about were God and their own country. They thought that they knew everything there was to know about Africa just by looking. They knew how poor people were and how wrong Africans were not to understand they were all the same since they were all black. I was Christian, and I had learned that all people were the same. It didn't matter to me whether they were white or black or green. However, there were other ways in which people were not all the same. I had been raised as a Nandi, and I had a lot of customs which couldn't be thrown away because of religion. Those customs were things which stuck to me as though I had been born with them. There were also things that it was not a sin to respect even if you were religious. For example, my people believed that if you were at the table eating, you should not talk while you were eating. If food was on the floor you shouldn't jump over it, but set it aside and then pass. Children also shouldn't eat with their parents at the table until they were 20 years old. Everyone had their own plates for food.

A custom which we didn't have which later took me a long time to learn was to compliment people on their food when you eat it. Food for my people was not something to get hysterical about. When someone gave you food to eat, you would never think it was something to thank them for. We felt that food was just there to be eaten and that tomorrow one would need to eat again. There was no reason to say anything because the food was not going to stay in your stomach for ever. My people thanked one another when a piece of art was given because that was something you could see for a long time. It also showed the person you thanked how you felt about their having gone to a lot of trouble to make something for you. Nandi are not a very emotional people, so there was always a limit to how much they could say thank you.

What I'm trying to say here is that customs of people are sometimes hard to get used to. During the time I was travelling with the missionaries, I often found myself in situations where I wouldn't know what to do. We would go somewhere, and the people there would make tea for us. While we were drinking the tea, the people who travelled with me told our hosts how good the tea was, but I always felt like a fool. I would never know what to say because the tea tasted just like any other tea.

I was with the Pentecostal Church for two years. Our pastor asked me if I was happy to continue with them as a witness. I said that I was. Then he asked me what I would think if they decided to send me to Finland to study so that when I came back I could be a fully-fledged missionary for them. I liked the idea of going abroad very much, but I had been with the Finnish missionaries for two years, and I was not crazy about going to their country. I told the pastor that I didn't have enough education to go to another country. He said that was the reason they wanted me to go there – to study. He told me that they would only teach me about the Bible, nothing else.

Although I knew that I didn't want to go, it was still nice to have been considered. I was proud of myself and went to tell my mother. I really knew that no matter how hard they asked me, I would never go, but I wanted to enjoy talking about it. I wanted my parents to know that I could go so far away that they wouldn't see me for ten years. It was good to see my mother look very worried for once. Next I went to my father to tell him. He told me that he thought it was dangerous to go far away without good security. I went to tell the church people that I couldn't go because my parents wouldn't let me. A girl from the town of Kisumu was chosen in my place.

That same year I decided to look for a real job. At that time a large

Coca-Cola bottling factory was being built in Kisumu, and I applied for a job there. I went to be interviewed and was given the job right away. The salary was good – 500 shillings per month. As the building wasn't completed I wouldn't start for another month. I decided to leave my work in the church to take a rest before starting the new job.

I had various relatives in Kisumu through my mother, and when I left the missionaries, I decided to move to my aunt's. My aunt Nur had seven daughters and one of them had just got married. She had married into a different Muslim sect, but otherwise the family were Ismailia Muslims. Aunt Nur made certain that all of the children went to the mosque every Saturday but she was really a Nandi in life-style. She was also a wonderful woman who never asked you to do anything if you didn't want to. She had married an Asian, and that was why she had become a Muslim. I didn't get along with her daughters very well because their way of life was so different from mine, and because they didn't speak Nandi.

One afternoon I decided to go downtown to do some window shopping. There was a large store with a lot of nice things to see, and I went inside to look around. I no sooner got in when a young man greeted me and offered to help me. I declined and said that I was just looking, but he didn't want to let me go. He kept showing me various things, and I could see that he wanted to talk to me. The manager of the store, an Asian, was watching him and finally asked him what I wanted. The man was terrified because he thought that his boss had noticed that he wasn't trying to sell anything to me. In his fear he told the boss that I was looking for a job.

'Why didn't you send her to me then?' the boss asked.

'Please tell him that you want a job,' the man begged.

I was shocked, not only because I didn't want a job at all, but also that shop was well known for not hiring African girls or ugly girls. However, I went up to the manager and he asked me what kind of job I wanted.

'I need a job as a salesperson,' I replied.

'Have you ever done sales work before?' he asked me.

I said that I hadn't. It was easy for me to say this because I knew I already had a job waiting for me. The man told me that he wanted to give me the job, but that he would have to try me out for two weeks to see how well I worked. If he thought my work was good after the two weeks, then he would hire me.

'If I work for you for two weeks on a trial basis, will you pay me for those two weeks if you decided not to hire me?' I asked.

'Don't worry,' he told me. 'I think that I will like your work. Just come tomorrow morning to start.'

I went home and discussed the matter with my aunt.

'There is no problem,' she told me, 'just go to work for him for two weeks and then tell him you have found another job.'

When I got to work the next morning the first thing I saw was the boss. He had a very fierce face, and I don't think he ever laughed more than once a week. That kind of face was very hard for me to understand. I asked him if he still wanted me to work for him.

'Of course,' he said, 'just come in.'

He told the other workers to show me what to do. All the people who worked for him were men, but that didn't bother me a bit. I have always been sure of myself, and never let anything intimidate me.

I worked all day long, and by the evening I was completely exhausted. There was a lot of standing but I enjoyed talking to the customers a lot. The only thing that was mysterious that first day was the boss himself. From the minute I entered the store he stared at me the entire day. He looked nasty even if he wasn't nasty. Later I knew why he was watching me; he wanted to make sure that I didn't steal anything. Finally I got fed up, I picked up my purse, went up to him and poured the entire contents out in front of him. Then I threw the purse to him. I asked him to go through it to see if he could find anything that had been stolen. If he could, he should call the police right away to take me to jail.

'What is all this about?' he asked.

'Why do you stare at me all the time?' I asked him. 'What do you think I'm doing? When I bend down, you bend down and stare at me. When I stand up, you do the same thing.'

'Why do you feel badly if I look at you and you know you are not a thief?' he said. 'Why should it bother you when I watch you while you are working?'

I told him that what bothered me was that I wasn't used to being stared at without any explanation. He said he was staring at me because he had told me he would watch me for two weeks to see if he liked my work. The funniest thing was that while he was watching me, the other employees (not Africans by the way) were stealing things to take to their girlfriends. I couldn't tell him that he had been watching the wrong person. But I had never stolen even a penny from anyone in my life. I told him that I had had enough of being watched and asked him to pay me for one week and let me go. He said that he couldn't do that because we had agreed that I would work for two weeks. I told him that was fair enough, and I worked out two weeks.

When the time was up he asked me what I was going to do and I told him that I had another job at the Coca-Cola factory.

'Do you have any idea of what they will pay you?' he asked.

'Yes, 500 shillings,' I said.

'Well, let me first tell you one thing,' he said. 'I have liked your work a lot, and I want to give you the job. Although I can't pay you that much money, I know that Coca-Cola job won't be a good one. Even if the salary is large, there is no guarantee that you won't just work for six or seven months and then get the sack. Let me give you my best offer and you can think it over.'

He offered me 250 shillings a month and a guarantee that I would have the job as long as I wanted.

I went home torn between the large salary and the secure job. Aunt Nur suggested I take the job with smaller salary because it was more secure and get my boss to put his guarantee in writing. Since I respected her, I followed her advice.

So I officially started my new job. The man was fierce as hot pepper. No one had ever worked for him for a full year. The people who were there when I started to quit after a few months. When this happened, my boss told me to go to look for a Nandi person like myself. In one year I managed to bring all of my cousins into the job, which helped a great deal. Every time he started in on one of us, we could talk about it among ourselves after work. We had three names we called him by. The first was 'hot pepper', next was 'lemon-face', and last was 'heart-trouble'. I now understood that the reason he told me he would never fire me was because he never fired anyone; instead people ran away when they could stand him no longer!

I ended up working with him for six and a half years. Nevertheless it took me a long time to know why he wanted Nandi like me. At first I thought he must like me a lot but that was not the case. A businessman like him never likes anyone or anything but money and himself. He would pretend that he liked you only as long as you brought him a lot of business. He was enthusiastic about me because he knew that I had the best personality for his business and that personality came with me as a Nandi person. No one in Nandi culture, however wealthy or respected he was, had the right to consider himself better than anyone else. We were all equals no matter what. I think that has made me sure of myself in life. I have never felt inferior to anyone at any time and I have been able always to talk to anyone without fear. The other side of the coin was that I never felt myself to be superior to anyone else. So when someone came into the shop, I never looked down on him or her but was always polite and nice and really meant it.

My boss used me like a washing-machine. When people came flooding to the store at the end of the month with their salary money, he stood at the door watching them. He had been in business all of his life, and he knew who had money and who didn't by the time they crossed the threshold. My section was normally material but at the end of the month I had to cover all departments: men's wear, ladies' wear, children's wear, plus modelling for the men who wanted to buy dresses for their wives. When a wealthy customer arrived, he would tell everyone in the store, 'Don't talk to that person, let Janie deal with him!'

While I was dealing with this person, someone else came in.

'I want to buy this dress, but I don't know how it's going to look on my wife,' the customer would say.

My boss would tell him to wait.

'Janie, can you come to try on this dress for this gentleman?' he called me.

My Christian name is Jane, but he called me Janie. Around the turn of the month I always felt like a hailstorm had just ended when evening came.

Another bad part of the job was that we were often only given 15 minutes to eat our lunch. Since I wanted to save my salary money, I didn't want to eat in restaurants, but 15 minutes is not enough time to cook a meal. The hours were also long. We began at eight in the morning and worked until six or six-thirty at night. This was every day except Sunday when we worked only half a day! Such greed for money I have never seen.

After six years I left Aunt Nur's and went to live on my own. I found a tiny house with just enough room for a bed. I had to cook outside, and then eat the food on my bed. All my dishes and clothing had to be stored under the bed. It was so small because I wanted to spend as little as possible on rent but I was happy because it was my own. I didn't have to show anyone where I lived. I would meet friends outside for lunch or to chat. My aunt alone knew where I lived. The place was built inside the courtyard of a large house which belonged to an Asian family. After a few months, the Asian women began asking me why I wasn't married.

'You don't go around with men. You are a very nice girl and lovely too. Lucky the man who is going to marry you. He will find a wonderful wife.'

In Africa, a girl who didn't run around with men was considered to be a good girl (especially by Muslims). I began to realise that I was not doing the right thing; the way I dealt with men was driving them towards me. They didn't know my reasons, but just assumed that I was saving myself for 'Mr Right' to come along. Every one of them tried to be 'Mr Right' for me.

Nevertheless even after I had realised that I didn't know how to deal with men, I remained the same. I was a child who had been raised by a single parent with stepmothers. I knew that there was no love in the world at all. I knew that the only one who really loved me was my father. Love from everyone else was just to get me to do something that they wanted. But although my father loved me a lot, there was still something missing. This was love from a mother. My stepmothers always treated me nicely only to please my father; they didn't love me themselves. I had tried to get my stepmothers to love me by doing all sorts of extra things for them. As a result I had the feeling that the only way to get someone to like me was to do something for them. If someone outside the family liked me, I thought they just felt sorry for me because I didn't have a mother. What made me feel even more strongly that there was no love in the world was realising how much my mother and father hated each other.

I never forgave myself when I remembered that I had to do something in exchange for someone's love. I was not rich, and I didn't think that I was good-looking or anything special. I felt like going out and telling the world to hate me or love me but that I would never do anything for anyone as long as I lived so that they would love me. I wanted to tell the world that it would see me the way I was for the rest of my life. I would never kid myself and get married thinking there was love. Love did not exist, and getting married was a waste of time which would only worsen one's situation.

After I had money enough to think that I could make it on my own, I became even more positive in thinking that I would never get married because I didn't want anyone thinking that my wealth came from the man I married. I had almost 10,000 shillings, and for me that was a lot. I felt like a millionaire, and in a sense I was. In those days land cost about 60 shillings an acre. I had calculated that 5,000 shillings would get me over 80 acres, and 4,000 shillings would get me about 20 dairy cattle. A thousand shillings would cover my expenses while I was getting ready.

I wrote to my stepsister telling her of my plan to buy a farm. When she got my letter she came to Kisumu and stayed with me for two months. During that time, she listened to my plan for only one day; the rest of the time she spent telling me how I didn't see the world in the right way. She tried to tell me that everything I thought was wrong was right. She tried to introduce me to good people. I would talk to them, and the next day she would ask me what I thought of them. I would tell her that I enjoyed talking to them, but that they were not on my mind today. After two months she gave up and went back home.

I was still working. I wanted to leave my job, but I had made up my mind to continue working for one additional year to get more money to buy my farm.

CHAPTER NINE
New Horizons

I had some friends who lived about 30 miles outside Kisumu. They only came to town a few times in a year, but they always visited me. Once one of these friends came to see me with a friend of his, Chet, a young student from North America who was studying languages in Africa. My friend had suggested he meet me as I spoke one of the dialects he was studying.

When they came into the shop, my friend told me that he wanted me to meet someone from our tribe. I looked at the newcomer. He was tall and thin, but I didn't understand what my friend meant; I knew that Nandi and Masai were tall and thin, but never white like this. I was introduced to Chet, and he tried to speak to me in my language. I couldn't understand a word! He had of course learned a different dialect from mine, and if you think it is difficult to understand someone who is just learning your language, imagine what it is like if the person is learning a dialect different from your own.

They were there about 20 minutes buying socks and talking to me. Since I had various religious friends, my boss thought Chet was one of them. He had asked my cousin who he was and she had told him it was a priest. After my friends left, he said, 'Is that a new priest, eh, Janie?'

I didn't understand what he was talking about, but my cousin gave me a signal, and I just agreed with him. On our way home I asked my cousin what the priest business was, and she said that when our boss had asked who Jane was talking to, the only thing that came into her mind to say was a priest. I began to wonder to myself. Maybe he really was a priest. He had certainly spoken very softly.

After a few months they came back again. This time we spoke only Swahili. We all became friends. After about a year, Chet asked me where I lived. I didn't want to tell him because I didn't want to break my custom of not telling anyone where I lived. Of course I didn't want to tell him that I didn't want to say, so the whole matter was a bit tricky. When he had left, I told myself that I had had a narrow escape.

He was gone for three months again, and people at work asked if the tall priest had gone back to his own country. I said I didn't know. One Sunday afternoon I was resting in my little house when I heard people running towards it. There were a number of high school girls who lived in the same building with me, and they were very excited. They told me that I had a visitor outside. I wondered who would excite them like this.

I went to the door, forgetting my shoes. When I opened it, something unusual happened to me: I ran out of words to say. Or rather I had too many things to say in my mind at once, and nothing could get out. I wanted to ask him how he had found my house, I wanted to say that I didn't know he was still in Kenya, and I wanted to say that it was nice of him to have come, but none of those words came out. I just opened the door and asked him right away what he wanted.

My girlfriends were horrified. They told me that was not a question to ask a visitor. I should ask the guest in first, and when he is in, ask him if he would like something to drink. Then it would be all right to ask him if there was anything he wanted. So I asked him in, and he said that he wasn't staying but had just stopped by to say hello on his way to do some work in the area. I asked him where exactly he was from, because I had never really been told, and in Nandi we don't usually ask men where they are from. I knew he wasn't British, but beyond that, nothing. He said that he came from North America. My goodness, I had heard about North America, but I had never seen anyone from there. I began to look at him in a different way.

In those days the only two places in North America that I had heard about were Washington DC, and California. Because Nixon was president of the United States then, and was from California, and because Hollywood was there, we all thought California was an incredible place where everyone was very rich, so rich that nobody drove Volkswagens there. So when I asked him what part of North America he was from and he said California I said 'Wow!' to myself. I wanted to ask him how much a lot of money was or what a lot of money looked like. I wanted to ask him if it was true that no one there drove little cars like Volkswagens. But he was in a hurry, and I was still recovering from realising that I had known someone from California for almost two years without being aware of it. I didn't mind his telling me he was going. In fact I was just waiting for him to go so I could call the other girls and tell them where he was from.

Everyone had a different question to ask. One asked what he had thought of Africa, another what America looked like, another if he had been to India. I told them that I hadn't asked any questions like that. They all thought I was a *kalulu* – someone who just sits and listens without a brain of her own. They asked me when he was coming back because they wanted to ask him things themselves. I told them I had no idea because he didn't come to Kisumu on my account, but to do work.

The next time Chet came, he told me that he would be going back to his country in a few months. I was a little upset, but I didn't see any point in telling him that. What I had enjoyed about knowing him was simply that he had liked my people and that he was a gentle person. I asked if he would write to me after he had gone, and he said he would. We talked a lot that day because it was his last chance to see me. He wasn't as happy as usual, and I felt that maybe he wanted to say something to me but wasn't willing to say it. Finally he said that there was something he had been wanting to ask me for a long time. He asked me if a white man wanted to marry me, would I marry him?

I wondered what he meant, but I decided that since he was about to leave anyway, there was no reason to tell him I didn't want to get married to anyone let alone a white man. Since I would probably never see him again, it was safe to say yes, and I did. I asked him if he knew a white man who wanted to marry a black woman, and he said that he didn't, he was only asking. He got up to go, and I gave him my address. I gave him my home address because I didn't know how long I would stay at my job.

I tried to carry on with the job, but I couldn't stand Kisumu any more. I didn't want to buy a farm now as I didn't feel I could cope with a completely new situation at that point. I wanted to go somewhere where I could stay and rest. Since the only thing I really knew was business, I decided to do that. I went up to Nandi to look for a shop to rent.

Very quickly, I found one in a place which was near neither my father nor my mother. My father by this time already owned several empty shops, but I didn't want to ask him for one because I knew that, although I would be given the building rent-free, he would make sure that my mother never came to visit me there. I wanted to be free from both of them and to have a place of my own. If my father wanted to come to see me, that would be fine, and if my mother wanted to come that was fine too.

After I had found the shop, I went back to Kisumu and told my boss that I was sorry but that I had to leave my job immediately. He asked me to reconsider for a week, and then see if I still wanted to leave. He thought that I only wanted more money, and in three days told me that he would increase my salary. I explained that the reason I was leaving was not because of money but because I was tired of being in Kisumu. He really wanted me to stay with him, but it was too late; I had made up my mind.

I bought supplies for my shop, and when everything was ready, I rented a truck to move everything. While I had been busy purchasing things, my friends had been helping to pack everything in the house.

When the truck was loaded I said goodbye to Kisumu. The truck arrived at my new shop in the afternoon and relatives were waiting there to help me unload everything. The only things I unpacked were my bed and my stove; everything else stayed wrapped up for three days. I just wanted to sleep, get up late at ten, take a bath and make my breakfast. After that I would take a blanket and spread it out on the hill behind my shop. I lay there on the ground and watched the grass blowing in the wind. There was a little river at the bottom of the hill, and when the wind blew the grass, I could see the water. When the wind died down, I felt nice and warm. The weather was perfect.

I was not completely new to the people in the area; almost everyone knew my parents, and so it was just like home. Those people who knew my parents well treated me like a little girl. For the three days I tried to rest they would come and ask me what the matter was. If I said that I was tired, some wanted to clean my shop for me, and others wanted to cook for me. The last thing I needed was for someone to come and mother me. I only needed to be alone for a few days.

On the fourth day I unpacked my goods to set up the shop. Everything from clothing to food was stocked in the shop; the only thing I didn't have was material. All my clothing was ready-made for men, women and children. In Kenya shops are not specialised like they are in other countries. If someone has a shop, she can sell anything she likes. That means that every shop is like every other shop, and the shopkeeper must work very hard to get people to come to buy at her particular shop. She has to do this by being extra friendly and nice to them.

Another difficult thing about owning a shop, especially in the country, was that people don't have very much money. You have to divide things into very small amounts. For example, sugar, salt and tea were sold in amounts ranging from a penny to a shilling. Even cigarettes couldn't be sold by the packet. You had to open a packet up and sell the cigarettes one by one. Initially this was a nuisance for me, but after a few months I got used to it.

The shop was located in a small village. There wasn't much business most days of the week. But on Wednesdays and Saturdays business was good because those were market days, and many people came into the village from the surrounding country. If you were well-stocked, on those days you could make about 700 shillings. (Pounds have never been used in Kenya.) The other days you would have to be content with about 25 pence if you were lucky. One nice thing about this situation was that on those slack days, I could just close the shop and rest. I started my shop with 5,000 shillings (now worth about 25,000 shillings), and by the end of a year, I had made a profit of about 4,000 shillings. I was pleased because in addition there had been plenty of time to rest. While I was there, I had made a number of nice friends. Two of my closer friends had problems. One had a husband who had taken all the money and left her with the children while he ran after women. The way this woman kept her children fed was by making and selling meat pies. Her children went to the bus stop and sold the meat pies to people who were arriving from anywhere. Although she was trying to keep her children alive doing this, it was hard for her. Like any business, sometimes things wouldn't go well, and if the meat pies weren't sold, then the children would eat them for their evening meal.

When someone is poor, people sometimes feel that something is wrong with her. The woman had borrowed money from everyone in the neighourhood until no one wanted to give her any more. Her problem was that sometimes when she borrowed the money, the meat pies wouldn't get sold, her children would eat them, and the next day she couldn't repay the people she had borrowed the money from and would even have to borrow from someone else. The poor woman could never get ahead.

When I found out about her problem, I felt sorry for her. Although I came from a rich family, I had learned myself that one had to struggle in this world as long as one lived. I was still struggling myself and didn't have much money to spare, but I felt that I had to do something to help her. One day I told her that I wanted to make an arrangement with her. I said that I would supply her with meat, flour, oil and spices for the meat pies, and then she would make them on Saturdays and Wednesdays and sell them in my shop on those days. I wouldn't take any profit, but would only cover my expenses. The woman was very happy when I told her about this plan. We worked that way for five months, and she got enough money ahead to make a go on her own. However, she continued to sell the meat pies in my shop. I didn't get a bad deal from the arrangement either. Her meat pies brought a lot of people into my shop to buy things.

My other friend was a little Asian girl, Mita, whose situation was similar to mine but worse. Her mother died when she was young and her father had hired a babysitter. After a year the little girl got sick and the babysitter suggested to the father that she stay overnight to look after the child and help the father out. The man thought that was very kind of the woman. The woman started staying overnight and after a few weeks it became apparent that she was there for good.

After that her life was miserable. The woman behaved like a were-wolf towards her. Everything in the house belonged to the woman now. The father had no idea what was going on. Whenever he came home, food was ready for him to eat, and a hot bath was waiting for him to jump right into. A man could not ask for more.

Mita was not affected in the same way that I was. She didn't feel negatively about love; she was looking for love so much that she didn't know the difference between being loved and being taken advantage of.

To make matters worse, the woman had persuaded the man to leave Kisumu and take them to the country. The father still worked in the city and came home only on weekends. The only time Mita had any relief was when she went to visit her father in Kisumu but those visits cost her dearly. The father lived with a bunch of young men, and the girl got pregnant after only two visits to Kisumu. She tried to hide it from everyone but her stepmother found out right away. She went around the whole neighbourhood spreading the news that Mita was pregnant. The woman made it even worse by saying that the father had got the girl pregnant. The neighbourhood was in a state of shock, and the father and the girl were made to look like animals because of the woman's gossip.

No one heard the story from Mita herself because she didn't talk about it. The Asians that I knew in Africa felt very badly when a girl became pregnant before she was married. If it happened they never talked about it. They tried to hide the girl until after the baby was born. The baby would be given away, and the matter never mentioned again by the family.

One day the woman saw me sitting on the step of my shop. She came to tell me the news which I had heard long ago.

'You seem like you don't get around much at all,' she said.

'No, I don't,' I replied.

'Well, you should get around more so you can learn about the people in the neighbourhood.'

'There is nothing for me to learn in this place,' I told her. 'I was born here, and everyone knows me.'

'Did you know your friend was pregnant?' she said.

'Yes I do know, and I think everyone else here knows too,' I said. 'The only person who wouldn't know here would be a deaf person.'

The woman didn't know how much I hated her. She reminded me of my stepmother who used to tell lies to my father about me. Because of that I have never been able to believe anything a stepparent says about a stepchild.

I couldn't talk to Mita any more because she felt as though she had been ostracised. Whenever I tried to get her attention, she walked away from me. I was very hurt that I couldn't help her. I only wanted to see her and tell her that I didn't believe what her stepmother was saying. She stayed inside a lot and only came out to wash clothes.

One day I went to Kisumu to buy supplies for my shop. When I returned in the afternoon, I saw the women of the neighbourhood gathered together talking among themselves. While I was unloading my car a friend of mine called to me.

'Tapsubei, what are you doing standing there? Something terrible is going on in that house,' she said to me.

'What?' I asked her.

'Mita is in labour, but her stepmother has refused to help her. She said that the only way she would help her was if the girl told her who the father of the child was.'

'I thought she knew who the father of the child was.'

I ran to her house right away. When I got there, the door was closed, and there was screaming inside. I forced my way in and saw Mita in a sagging bed trying to push the baby out. She would push once and then scream. Her face had turned red.

When I saw her, I was very nervous and afraid that she was going to die. I couldn't see any sign of a baby. The girl's stomach was very small, and to make matters worse, she was screaming, 'the baby, the baby'.

I asked her if the baby was still in or if it was out. She said that it was still in. I made her sit against a wall so she would have something to lean against. When I finished positioning her, I came around in front to hold her legs steady so that she could push. In half an hour, the baby was out. It was a baby boy, but I didn't know if he was alive. He had just dropped down on to some rags. I put him in front of the girl. He was silent for a few seconds, but then he cried. As soon as he cried, I sprinkled a little water on his face, and cut and tied his umbilical cord. Then I wrapped him in a blanket and put him in the sagging bed. While I was doing this, Mita's stepmother had come back and was standing at the door watching me without a word. I didn't care, but just went on with my job.

I asked Mita to push the placenta out. She pushed for two minutes, but nothing came. I began to panic; I knew that if it didn't come out, the girl would die and the nearest hospital was a long way away. I remembered I had been told in such a situation to slip a chain down the mother's throat. This would make her gag and throw up, which would force the placenta out. I had a necklace made of chain which I let down the girl's throat. In one minute the placenta was out.

I was so relieved and excited I wanted to hug someone to say I was so glad that everything had turned out well. I ran to the door and hugged the stepmother. When I saw her face, I almost said, 'Sorry, I didn't mean to hug you.'

When I was ready to leave, the woman said something incredible.

'Since you have done everything else, why don't you wash the floor?'

'I'm sorry,' I told her. 'If you can't stand it, you can wash it yourself or leave it for the girl's father to wash.'

All the women in the neighbourhood came to thank me for having had the courage to help Mita. The next day her father arrived from work in Kisumu. Before he went home, the women in the neighbourhood ran and told him he should thank me first. They told him that if I hadn't been around, his child might be dead.

A few minutes later, there was a man at my door with a very long beard, frightening to look at. I didn't recognise him as Mita's father as I'd never seen him up close. I asked him what he wanted. He told me he was the girl's father. When he came in he bent down and touched my feet and cried.

'I don't know how to thank you for saving the life of my child,' he said.

I tried to explain to him that I hadn't saved her life for her own sake alone really. I was trying to do something for someone whose life, without her real mother, was very similar to mine. When I helped her, I had felt almost as though I was helping one of my sisters.

Although I was a complete stranger, the man was open with me. He spent hours telling me about the problems he had been through because of his wife. He said he was only waiting for his daughter to have the baby, and then they would leave together. He asked if I would help him once more. He asked me whether I would be prepared to take the child. I wanted to help him a lot, but that was a big step for me to take.

All of this time I had been keeping in touch with Chet. At the beginning there was no plan for me to go to North America. Then I met an American woman named Margaret McPherson who was dating an American doctor. I told her about my friend, and she said, 'Well, since you want to study so much, why don't you ask him in your next letter to see if he can find an opening for you in a school where he is?' So I wrote to him and told him about that and told him that I had saved enough money to go but that I wondered if going was worthwhile. First he wrote back and said that he didn't have a job, but that he would look for a school for me. He himself was planning to come to Africa. Despite this, my hopes and thoughts about going to North America to study were high.

According to my baptismal certificate, I was 23 years old and I felt I had a lot of time left to study. I wasn't thinking of children in those days, and when the man asked me to take the baby, I didn't know what to do. I liked children a lot, but this was not the time. I asked him to give me a week's grace to think. As soon as the man left, I sent a telegram to my mother to tell her about my problem.

When mother got my telegram, she was really shocked. She thought I had gone mad and wrote to me immediately. This was her letter.

Dear Tapsubei,

Thank you for letting me know what you almost ran into. I think you really need my help, and I'm glad that you asked for it. I know that you are very good and willing to do things for people who are in trouble, and I'm very glad that you helped that little girl. However, I don't think you should do any more than you have already done. You must think about what will happen to you if that man dumps all of his problems on you to save his daughter from embarrassment. When they leave, his wife will find out that you knew her husband and were planning things with him. If that ever happens, I'm sure that woman will kill you.

Love, Mother

Mother's letter was very strong. I didn't know what to say to the man. If I was to have the child, it wouldn't be to please him but to please myself and the child. I decided I would take the child, but not the money.

There were still three days left to tell him my decision. One thing I was clear about was that the man and his wife would have to agree about giving me the child. Then if the wife found out, I wouldn't have to move, and I wouldn't be killed if I stayed. After that, the man could arrange himself about going away with his daughter.

My mother didn't believe I would get out of the mess myself. She came to make sure that I didn't do something I would regret later on. She told me that what I wanted was too dangerous. I told her that I had dreamt of how I would raise the child. I wanted to raise him to be the finest man in the world. I wanted to watch him grow up and educate him as much as possible. Then one day I would tell him the story of what was happening right now. When my mother saw how I felt about the child she told me that she wasn't going to try to ruin everything for me if I really wanted to have it. But she insisted that, if the man and his wife wanted me to have the child, they ought to do it in the proper way.

'I know it sounds nice to you now when you are being told that you will get a child,' she said. 'But I should tell you that raising a child without a father is very hard. You may think that the only reason they are giving you the child is embarrassment because the mother was not married. However, there is another reason: they know that the girl would not be able to take care of the child without a husband.'

The man came to my house on Monday, and I introduced him to my mother. He sat down, and now Mother took control. She and I have different ways of dealing with delicate situations. For myself, if I know that the things I'm going to say are negative, I always start with the reasons first. That way I feel that the person won't be hurt as much as they would be if I told him the bad news first.

Mother is not like that. If there is bad news, she will just say it right away with no beating around the bush. She said she wanted him to have his wife and daughter there too and then we could have a proper discussion. There was nothing the man could do but go to get his family. He knew that his wife would be happy to have the baby given away as long as she didn't know that after the baby was gone, the man and his daughter were leaving too.

Mother made sure the man understood one additional thing before he left.

'You have to understand if we are lucky enough to have the baby that I will be the one who will keep him, not my daughter. She is not married either and doesn't know where she will be next year, and she is still my responsibility.'

An hour later the whole family arrived. The discussion started again, but since the man hadn't told his wife anything. He started to explain the situation to her there, but he didn't tell her the truth. He told her that he wanted Mita to give the baby away so that the whole family could move back to Kisumu. His wife, however, didn't like the idea. She didn't want to leave her house here and go back to the city.

Mother told them to go home and agree among themselves first. She gave them her address in Nairobi, and told them that she was sorry but she had to get back to her job. She told them that if they decided they wanted us to have the child, they should contact her and not me because she didn't want me to have a child without a husband. On Wednesday she went back to her job. The man and his daughter were there for a week longer. After that I didn't see them. They had left without telling anyone where they were going, and I never heard from them again.

Now that the incident with the baby was over I carried on with my life. My shop was growing bigger. Although I was still not certain whether I would go to North America, I was working hard to earn money in case I decided to go. I wrote again to Chet to find out for sure if I would be able to go to school if I went abroad. He didn't reply for a month, and I began to put all thoughts of hearing from him out of my mind. Finally his letter came; he had finished his PhD degree and had taken a job in south-western Ontario in a country called Canada. He said it was a good place and that I would be able to study there. Chet had written to me from several different places since he had left Africa, and I had the feeling that he would never stay in one place. I wondered what would happen if I were to go to where I thought he was and find that he had moved on.

However, I realised that if I didn't go this time, I might not ever get another chance. I wanted to see the rest of the world very badly and I now had enough money to get there. I wouldn't sell my shop but would leave it for my mother to run for me. If something went wrong, then I would have a place to come back to. I called my mother to come to look after the shop while I took a little holiday. I didn't dare to tell her I was leaving the country because I knew that if I did, she would become hysterical.

As soon as my mother arrived, I left for Nairobi to get a passport. I found out that I needed a birth certificate and a medical check-up. I returned to Nandi country because my birth certificate had to be signed by people who knew my date of birth.

When I was born, people had children at home, and no one remembered exactly when a child was born. There were no important ceremonies accompanying birth. The birthdays of nearly everyone in Kenya, and perhaps most of Africa, from my generation and earlier are made up. Occasionally your parents might remember the year you were born in, but they wouldn't remember the month or the day. My baptismal card said that I was born in 1950, but that was a guess. I decided to make my date of birth earlier so there wouldn't be any question about my being allowed out of the country. I went to see a doctor to get my form signed and when I was asked what year I was born in I said 1942.

The doctor stood up and looked at me.

'You look like a person who was born in 1949 or 1950,' he said, 'not someone who was born in 1942.'

He said that he wouldn't give me an official birth certificate, but would give me a form for my parents to sign saying I was born in 1942.

I went to see father. I told him I needed to get a birth certificate and that I didn't want to be any younger than twenty-five or twenty-six years old. I was very worried father would ask me why I needed a birth certificate in the first place and why I was so concerned about my age. He asked me to choose between twenty-five and twenty-six. I chose the latter.

'All right,' he said. That means you were born in 1946. Any special month and day?'

I chose 15 January. Father never even asked me what this was all about.

I went back to Nairobi and started the endless runaround of passports and vaccinations. A friend, John, who knew all the ins and outs, helped me. When my passport was finally ready I was told that anyone who was going abroad alone had to post a bond of 5,000 shillings. I asked John whether I would ever get the money back. He told me that I would be given documents and receipts indicating that the money would be reimbursed when I returned. I had no other choice but to trust him, and of course he was absolutely correct. Although it was to be many years before I saw that money again, when the time came to get it, I had no trouble at all.

In three weeks everything was ready. I sent a telegram to Chet, and the next day he called John's office. John asked me if I wanted to talk to him, but I didn't. There were so many problems on my mind that I didn't know what to tell him. He was just calling to find out when I would be arriving in Toronto and to let me know that the plane might stop in Montreal first and that I shouldn't get off there even though it was Canada.

There were three days left now before I was to leave Kenya. I went back home to say goodbye to my parents. Both were shocked, but no one thought of asking me why I was going. They both just wanted to know when I would be coming back. I told them I would write to them after I had arrived and knew when I would be returning.

I left home for Nairobi at four in the morning and arrived twelve hours later. The plane was to leave at eight o'clock that night. I went to my cousin's house and packed my clothes. By six o'clock I was ready, and I was taken to the airport. While I had been away, my friends had decided to make a surprise party for me to be held at the airport. On the way to the airport, I told John and his wife how I wished I'd had time to say goodbye to so-and-so and so-and-so. They said not to worry because I could write to them after I had arrived. When I got to the airport, everyone I had wanted to say goodbye to was there, including one of my younger brothers. There were almost 40 people, and we partied until seven-thirty. Then the passengers were told to board the plane.

'You are really going for good now,' John said to me. 'Now is the time for you to say goodbye to all of us.'

I didn't want to say goodbye, and I began to feel badly about leaving my people. John took me near to the door, but he didn't say goodbye to me.

'You have to know that you are on your own now because in the country you are going to you won't have your people to stand by you if anything goes wrong,' he said. 'Look after yourself well, and we will keep in touch with you.'

I got on to the plane feeling very lonely. I felt lonely for two hours, and then I told myself I could make it on my own. All of the people who were sitting around me knew my name. When we left the airport terminal to board the plane my friends and relatives had gone to the roof of the terminal and yelled down to me, 'Tapsubei, goodbye, Tapsubei,'

The passenger next to me behaved as though he had known me for generations. He kept ordering whisky and trying to persuade me to have the same. I told him that I didn't drink alcohol but that didn't stop him from asking. As soon as he had finished one drink, he would call for another and ask me again. After three times, I said I didn't have any money. That was the wrong answer because he then said, 'No, this one is on me.'

We landed at Rome in the early morning. I asked the customs official to show me how to get to immigration. He pointed to a sign marked immigration, but I couldn't see how to get there. What I could see was an escalator coming down. I had never seen an escalator before, and wondered how in the world I was going to get up it. I couldn't ask anyone because no one seemed to speak a language I could understand.

I asked myself what in the world would make people build a device which made it harder to get to the immigration section. After twenty minutes, I still had not seen anyone going up the escalator, only people coming down. The loudspeaker announced the arrival of a plane for Canada and instructed people to go to their sections. I couldn't wait any longer. I tried to hang on to the railing, but it pushed me back down. I could hear voices laughing behind me, but I didn't dare look back; I thought that the minute I took my eyes off the escalator, I would be hurt. Finally as the escalator brought me down, someone took my hand and pulled me back. I think he was trying to tell me I was on the wrong side of the escalator, but since he was speaking Italian, I didn't understand what he was saying. I thought I had done something wrong, and that he was taking me to the police.

I decided to tell him what I thought before he got me to the police station.

'It doesn't matter if you think I have done something wrong,' I said. 'The person who built that escalator built it in the wrong direction. The sign for immigration is up, and the escalator is going down.'

'It is all right, come,' the man said to me.

His English was poor, and mine was too. I didn't understand why he was telling me it was all right.

He took me to the correct side of the escalator and left. I stood wanting to ask if I was free. When I got to the top of the escalator, I went to immigration and gave the officials my passport. They stamped it and returned it to me. I opened it to see if they had indicated that I had done something illegal. What I saw was only a stamp showing that I had passed through immigration in Rome. I jumped for joy when I realised I was free and had done nothing wrong.

The trip to Canada was very pleasant. When we got to Toronto I thought I was used to lines of officials by then but since I was staying in Canada, I was asked many more questions than I had been in Rome.

However, everything went well, and when I had finished I collected my baggage and went through customs. I didn't have very much with me, but the man who checked my luggage was fascinated with every little thing I had brought with me from Africa. He asked me about everything he wasn't familiar with. Finally he found a cooking spice (cardomon) that he knew himself. He was amazed that we would have the same thing in Africa. He started telling me what it was used for in Canada and even seemed surprised when I told him that we, too, used it in cooking. Finally he finished with me, and I went out and waited until Chet arrived.

CHAPTER TEN
Impressions of Canada

It was autumn when I arrived in Canada and the leaves were beginning to turn colour. They were golden-yellow and red-orange to match the sun and the sunset. This I had never seen. Travelling from Toronto to London, Ontario, there were miles of bare space without any houses. Then all of a sudden there would be lots of houses. People seemed only to live in towns, not spread out evenly over the country the way the Nandi were. It was surprising to me that the only smoke I saw came from factories and never from people's houses. Usually when I saw smoke from a chimney it made me feel happy because our houses always had smoke coming from the chimney in the morning and in the evening. The Nandi's favourite animal was the cow, and I wanted to see a farm as soon as I could. I was shocked to see the cattle chased like dogs. The people from the towns, I learned, were afraid of cattle and tried to run away from them when they came close. With us, cattle are almost like people. When they are young they stay in our houses, and we give them names which they keep all their lives. Each cow knows its own name.

I was impressed most of all by the size of the houses. Two people would live in a huge house! I thought it was a waste for a couple to live in a three- or four-bedroom house. I liked the neatly mowed lawns. In fact the neatness and cleanness of everything impressed me very much.

It was good to see Chet again. We got to London about six o'clock and I was very hungry. Chet said we would have something new to eat, that we didn't have in Africa and we went out to order it. After only a few minutes it was ready. A girl brought something in a flat box, gave it to Chet, he paid and we left. I wondered whether the food was fresh or just left-overs. I didn't say anything because I didn't want him to think I thought he didn't know what he was doing but in my own mind I had already decided that we had been given left-over food to eat. The reason I thought this was because when we cooked in Africa it usually took about five hours to prepare. If we were really rushing it might be three hours. I had never heard of a meal that only took ten minutes to get ready.

When we got home, we unpacked the food. It was pizza. Chet took a bite and pronounced it good. He asked me what I was waiting for. I didn't like the smell of the food. It smelled like something about to be spoiled. I took a small piece and an even smaller bite. The cheese on the pizza tasted spoiled. I said that I really wasn't hungry at all because we had eaten in the plane just before landing. In my mind I decided that I would have to make chicken or something else really nice for him so he could learn what real food tasted like. After the pizza we made tea. The tea tasted funny too. I was tired and went to bed early. The apartment was a one-bedroom basement apartment with only a single north-facing room. The sitting-room and the kitchen were open to each other. So Chet took the sitting-room and I took the bedroom. We thought we could do this for a few weeks until I found a place of my own to stay. But when it came down to it, my money was not enough. I had only a few thousand dollars, and Chet only had a job, but no money saved. So the result was that we shared the apartment, each person contributing to the rent and food.

I woke up at ten the next morning and Chet had gone to work. I took a bath, made breakfast and went back to bed. I made my breakfast in the style I had seen the British having when I babysat for them. I hadn't learned about the North American style of having a candy bar for breakfast yet! I had two pieces of toast, two eggs, orange juice and tea. The only thing that was missing was the bacon. (Looking ahead I can tell you that I arrived from Africa weighing 95 pounds and in a short time was up to 120 because of these breakfasts. This made me really happy since I had been trying for years to put on weight.)

When Chet returned at three, he rushed into my bedroom to wake me up because he thought I had been sleeping since last night. He asked me if I would like to meet some friends of his, I said yes, and we went. The people were our age and were very nice. They told me about a place where I might be able to study and we went the next day and talked to the head of the school. I was admitted, but I had to wait for six weeks because I was late for the current cycle of classes. I was elated.

Now I wanted to shop for the chicken. First I needed some spices. I wanted fresh coriander, garlic, onions, tomatoes and curry powder. I found everything except the coriander which was simply nowhere around. The next morning I set the chicken on the stove to cook. I kept adding water until three o'clock when I thought it ought to be ready. When I put a fork into it, to my astonishment, it fell apart. All I had was a thin gruel; the chicken had completely disintegrated! I was shocked. What had I done to it? There went the dinner for that night. There was no way to put the pieces back together again. I had intended it as a surprise, but when Chet came in, I had to tell him right away what had happened. He explained to me that although in Africa a chicken had to be cooked for five hours before it was tender enough to be chewed, the chickens here weren't allowed to run around free and get tough like the African ones. That night we ate out again. It turned out to be my introduction to fast food. We went to McDonalds, and I thought it was super. For the next few months anytime going out to eat was mentioned, I would pop up with McDonalds.

While I was waiting for my school to start I couldn't go anywhere by myself because of the language problem. I could understand people, but they couldn't understand me very well, and then they would shout at me as though I were deaf. I didn't enjoy that. I often stood at the window and counted the cars passing by. In my village in Africa, a car was a rarity. Although we had buses and trucks, the roads weren't paved, and a passing vehicle just meant a lot of dust.

When I got tired of this, I would walk to the university and back, a distance of about a mile. It surprised me that with such a lovely paved road, there were so few people walking on it. I was frightened – maybe there was something dangerous along the way. In the evening, however, if I went for a walk, people would be out running and jogging. It seemed crazy to me to drive a mile to work and then run after driving back from work. Later I learned that running and walking were not considered ways of getting somewhere in North America, but as medication to be taken on the advice of a doctor.

As the days passed by, I learned more about living in the Western world. In many respects it appeared to me much as I had imagined it. Because people had so much, it never occurred to me that anyone might steal something. I trusted everyone I met. One day I took my clothes to the laundry room, loaded them into the washing-machine and left them there. Later when I removed my things some of my African material was missing. Someone had come, opened the machine, picked out the African cloth and left the other clothing. I didn't think it had been stolen until Chet came home. When I told him it was missing, he said he was sorry that he hadn't told me not to leave clothing lying around unattended because it might be stolen.

I was flabbergasted. I couldn't imagine that in a rich country like this, people would steal something like cloth. With my people it would be very embarrassing to steal clothing even though many individuals don't have much of their own. If someone were to be found stealing clothing who was Nandi, we would take him to a mental hospital.

Although I couldn't understand why anyone would take someone else's clothing, I had learned my lesson. I never left clothes alone in the laundry room. After a while, however, I began to get tired of this and decided it was probably safe to leave everything but African cloth. I was wrong, and in a few days some towels were taken. I was never careless again.

I was very impressed when I went shopping. In Africa, in a store owned by an Asian, when you go in to buy something, it will have a price ticket of say 100 shillings. You ask its price, and are told, '100 shillings, how much do you have?' You pretend to leave and say, 'I don't have enough.' The Indian will ask you, 'Do you have 60?' You say, 'I only have 40,' and walk out. The Indian chases you down the street saying, 'All right, bring your money then. Let me go broke.' You buy it and feel like you have got a good bargain. In Canada, when I asked the price after looking at the ticket, I was always told exactly the same price! I would say, 'Oh no! I don't have that much!' Nobody would say anything. Then I would walk away, and still no one would run after me trying to get me to buy. In fact it was, and is, often impossible to get someone to help me with a purchase whereas in Africa, the Asian shopkeepers snatch you at the door.

After I had been in Canada for a month, a Thanksgiving meal was given by one of Chet's colleagues. This was my first opportunity to attend a Western 'ceremony', in this case a feast. There was little that I saw, however, that could be classified as ceremony. There was only a lot of food and a lot of eating. The first thing that impressed me was the way the food was decorated; I had a hard time telling what was to be eaten from what was just decoration. While I was still wondering about this, a large dog came along. In Africa no one would let a dog in when food was laid out for eating. When I saw the dog jumping over some food, I wanted to tell someone to let it out but before I could do this, the person sitting next to me started petting the dog. I asked myself how she could do this when food was all over the place. The dog's hair would get into the food. Then the dog's owner started petting the dog and the dog licked her mouth. She laughed and kissed the dog back. I couldn't believe what I was seeing. I had to pinch myself to make sure I wasn't dead or dreaming. Now I have nothing against dogs, but I have never thought that a dog was more than a dog. People related to dogs by giving them food in my world, but not as a relative or a boyfriend or girlfriend.

Finally the tables were all arranged, and we prepared to take the food outside. I was in real trouble because I couldn't refuse the food by saying I had already eaten. The food looked so inviting, but I couldn't think of eating when I remembered the dog. I sipped soft drinks until the desserts, which had been kept separately, were laid on the tables. Those I could eat. After eating everybody started giving one another compliments and congratulations about the food.

The people were completely different from me. They were behaving now in ways I had long grown out of. A husband and his wife started hugging and kissing in front of other people. When I tried to think why they were doing that, I couldn't come up with any reason. We used to do that when we were children of 14 or so years in front of other children. Maybe it felt nice for them to do it front of people.

Meanwhile other people had gone into a little forest near the house. It was autumn, and all of the leaves on the trees had turned red and yellow. When these people returned they were carrying little pieces of rock they had picked up. They thought the rocks were 'fascinating'. Others who had gone into the forest talked about the trees with their coloured leaves.

When I heard their conversation I was confused. Their discussion of how nature fascinated them took me back to when I was eight years old, and we talked exactly like that. We had all grown out of those things, however. Perhaps since I had grown up in the country, nature was not something amazing to me.

The women who were there didn't look to me as though they were having a very good time, although some of them put on a good show of kissing and hugging. At that time I didn't think that meant anything. It didn't occur to me that maybe that was just their custom. Eventually I came to wonder why wives even went to parties at all because they never seemed to enjoy themselves. They even didn't seem to enjoy talking to other women, but just spent their time trying to hang on to their husbands. I had been told Canada was a land of freedom for everybody, but when I saw how the women and the men were behaving and struggling with one another, I didn't see any freedom there. Actually, when the men sat down with their wives to talk, the men controlled the conversation because they spoke a different language. I suspected that the language was the one they used in their work because when the men talked, the women didn't have very much to say. However, they couldn't give up trying to participate in the conversation. Since the men were all university teachers, maybe the problem was exaggerated on that account.

After I had been in Canada for only three months, it seemed to me that things were getting worse for me instead of better. I was trying very hard to make myself think like the people here and appreciate their ways. When the weekend came we used to go to the park. I always had a good time with the children there. They seemed more real and more alive than their parents. Sometimes, however, things would happen which I wasn't prepared for. When I saw a mother swinging on the children's swing instead of her child, then I would become bewildered again. Other times I would see the whole family, father, mother and children together eating ice-cream. With my people, adults never eat sweet things, especially men. When I saw this I decided I wasn't crazy; I had just come from people with very different customs.

A person growing up in Nandi is taught to adapt herself to the ways of the people where she is so that she doesn't look like she is trying to appear smarter than they are. We say, 'If you go to a cannibal's house, you have to learn to be a cannibal yourself.' My problem with following this advice in North America was that in Nandi there are three clear stages in a person's life: childhood (where anything goes), initiation (when the laws of adult life are learned) and adulthood (when the ways of children are left behind and one lives according to the laws for the rest of one's life). North Americans are not initiated, and they never stop living and behaving like children. But I myself couldn't go back to my childhood since I had already been initiated.

My six weeks of waiting were finally up, and I started school. I travelled by bus to school during the day, and in the evening Chet came to pick me up. Everyone in the school was from a different country. There were both girls and boys. Although no one was from Kenya, it was much better being with them. We all had something in common. Some people were seeing strange things like me, and others were experiencing discrimination. The people who were most affected by discrimination were Asians from Uganda. When they lived in Africa, they had called themselves white; in Canada they were considered to be black or coloured, and they didn't like it.

We girls talked a lot about boyfriends since we were all there alone without our families to talk about. Each of us kept an eye open to find someone. I had a Hungarian girlfriend Lisa and various other friends as well. Lisa found a boyfriend before me. His name was Ambrose. Finally I found one. He was Iranian. We girls never took our boyfriends home with us because we all stayed with other people. Similarly the boyfriends lived with other people. So they were mostly school and early-evening-after-school friendships. It happened that Chet found out about this one day when Lisa came to visit me and we were arranging to go to a dance. When he heard us talking about a dance, he asked me if he could take me himself. I said, 'What about Lisa?' He said he would pick up Lisa's boyfriend too. So we ended up going as a foursome. We had a good time, and after that Chet and I decided to do other things together. We took dancing lessons and went to the theatre and the movies. Finally, we decided to become boyfriend and girlfriend, at least for the time I was to be here.

I spent two years in school, and after that it was time for me to go back home. But it was too late; I had stayed with Chet too long. We both realised that it was not going to be easy for either of us. Instead of my leaving, we decided to get married. No one else knew anything about this. We just went out and got a marriage licence and then called some friends and asked them to be our witnesses.

In my culture there are many ceremonies, and each ceremony has many stages. The person who is your witness or sponsor in a ceremony teaches you about these before the ceremony. With this in my mind, I asked my friend if there was anything I should know about the ceremony the next day. She said no, there wasn't much to it, really. The minister would read to me, ask me to repeat what he said, put the rings on me and my husband, and then I would kiss my husband and it would be finished.

I wondered to myself if what we were going to do was to be read to us by someone, why we couldn't just buy the marriage book and read it to ourselves. After I got home, I asked Chet if all marriage ceremonies were the same in English culture.

'If you know how to read from a book yourself, why do you want someone else to read to you?' I asked him.

He said that was just part of the ceremony. If you read the ceremony to yourself and said that you were married, that was not enough. I didn't want to ask any more, but I wondered what the minister was going to add to the book when he read it that was so important.

The marriage took place at ten the next morning. It was pretty much what I had been told it would be except at the end when we were both asked to make a vow. My husband was asked first, and he answered right away. Then it was my turn, and I hesitated. If I hadn't done this, the ceremony would have lasted only two minutes, but since I did, it lasted a little longer. I didn't understand why I was being asked to swear that what I was doing was what I wanted.

In my culture the only thing one is ever asked to swear in a ceremony is that you will keep the secret parts of the ceremony secret. The women don't want the men to know their ceremonies and vice versa, So if the minister had asked me to swear that I would never repeat to anyone what we had just done, I would have agreed immediately.

After we left, I felt that I had been asked to make a meaningless vow. There is no divorce in Nandi, so when you are getting married there is no reason to make any kind of vow. Before a man and a woman get married, they are given a lot of time to learn what marriage really means. Like any woman I had been taught that when I got married I would be in love, but that I should be prepared not to live on that dream because it wouldn't last for very long. We are prepared by being told that marriage is as much struggle as love. Men are taught by other men who are married. The first thing they are told is that they must stay away from the kitchen and never mess the house. If they want to stay out of trouble, they shouldn't touch anything after it has been arranged by their wives. Sometimes our teachers made marriage sound worse than it really was. After all of this, there was certainly nothing to swear for, and we knew for sure that there was no divorce. For a woman there was only one husband in one life. Even if you were separated from your husband for 20 years, you would still be married at the end of all that time.

After we got married, we decided to look for a place in the country. We got one on condition that we did not have any children. We stayed there for three years until our son was born in 1977.

After I had been in Canada for five years, we went to a meeting on African linguistics in Michigan. There I met some fellow Africans, including Maina and Kimalel, a man from my own tribe who had been in America for four years. There were Kenyans with him from other tribes as well. We had a lot of experiences to share. I especially wanted my fellow Nandi to help me understand what I had observed about life over here and to tell me if he had noticed the same things.

We first talked about people in general, and I told them how rare it was for me to see someone with a really happy face. I said that when people here talked it often seemed they were competing to see who was most clever. I was told that what I had seen was true, but that it was true all over the world, not just here, that city people think they are more clever than everyone else. That helped me a lot to understand.

Kimalel said he couldn't understand why people couldn't both be clever and have a sense of humour at the same time. I said that I had been wondering about the same thing in Canada for five years. For Americans, I thought I had part of the answer. If an American had a bit of humour, he would sell it to Hollywood; there certainly wasn't any left anywhere else. I had the feeling that nothing was free in America. If you wanted to laugh, then you had to pay for it.

Kimalel had a problem he thought I might be able to help him with. He was involved with an American girl. At first he didn't know how serious it was, but then he found himself deeply in love with her. The girl loved him too, and finally she moved in with him. They lived together for a few months, but then things started to get hard. Kimalel was a graduate student, and he was trying to finish his master's degree. He had a lot of work to do, but at the same time he was having to learn how to live with a white girl. She complained if he brought work home with him and claimed he didn't love her any more. He didn't know what to say because his feelings towards her hadn't changed but he was concerned to get his work done. As a Nandi man, he had been taught since he was little not to argue with a woman. The girl was always hurt because whenever she asked him to discuss things with her, he would have nothing to say. Kimalel was beginning to think that being in love with a white person was too demanding. He told me all this because he thought I might be able to help him since I was married to a white man. Unfortunately I couldn't. I had to tell him that my husband sometimes made me feel exactly the same way. When he came home from work, if the food wasn't ready, he would often go right away to his study.

Maina's story was different. He seemed to have known about the things that bothered Kimalel before he came to America. What was bothering him now was the necessity of speaking positively about everything. He said that the second day of his arrival he was taken to a symphony. The music was so depressing to him that he promptly fell asleep. The only time he woke up was when people clapped their hands; when they stopped, he went back to sleep. Finally after clapping the people got up from their seats. It was over! As soon as they had stepped out of the hall, his hosts asked him how he had liked it.

Maina said that he had to think a little bit before he answered. One thing he was sure of was that he never wanted to hear that kind of music again. But he didn't want to say that the music sounded miserable because he didn't want to be impolite. Eventually his dislike of the music was stronger than his wish to be polite, and he told his hosts that not only had he not liked the music, but he had slept through the whole performance. Saying that was one of the most painful things he had ever done, and he wished that people would not ask for compliments at all.

Maina also had problems dating. If he went out with a girl for even a few dates, the girl would always ask him if they were going to 'go steady'. Not wanting to take a chance, Maina always answered no.

By the time I had finished listening to them, I knew that their problems had to do with girls more than anything else. However, the time was not wasted as I learned a lot from them. I asked them about the women's movement in America. They told me that women had plenty of freedom and were asking for more. However, they didn't know how to use the freedom that they already had; they just used it to drive themselves and their husbands crazy. I should have realised they were men before I asked because now our conversation turned into a disagreement. They said that women didn't really need equal rights. Instead of using their freedom to get out and do whatever they wanted, they used it to make their husbands do housework even though the wife was not working. They thought that men in North America had a much worse deal than women. If they had been North American men, they would have argued that there were only two alternatives for the women: either they should have men's jobs and let the men stay home to take care of the house and children, or a law should be passed saying that husbands and wives shouldn't live in the same house. When a man and a woman got married, they said, they should decide right away if they wanted to have children. Then when the woman was pregnant, the man would support her until she had her baby. Once the baby was born, the couple would decide who would have the first baby. If the father was to have it, they would work out a deal for the wife to look after it until a second child had been born. At that point the husband could take his child, and the wife would be left with hers. Kimalel and Maina thought that would provide the most freedom for both of them. The children would be free to visit each other any time they wanted to. The freedom of living in separate houses would give everyone real equality.

I understood their point. Women shouldn't ask for more equality if that freedom is doing miserable things to their marriages. But that was not my question. I was asking why the girls they knew were so anxious about how the men felt towards them if they were really free. I had thought that freedom was something to make a woman sure of herself. I was a little disappointed that they saw things so one-sidedly. I knew that if I said that, in my opinion, the women weren't to blame alone, an all-night disagreement would ensue. Nevertheless, I didn't want them to get away with thinking that I went along with everything they had said. Just before they left, I said it had been nice talking to them, but why was it that, whenever something is wrong, it's the woman's fault all over the world? I didn't expect an answer but I wanted them to know that I didn't think everything was women's fault.

CHAPTER ELEVEN
Men and Women, Young and Old

Back in Canada I decided to go back to school in order to meet new people, and my husband suggested that I take a typing course. I met a lot of women and I found they were really fine people except that they were wrapped up in their own worlds. They talked most about what they did with their husbands and what they were going to be doing with them the next week. My husband didn't appear to do any of the things that theirs did for them. After I had learned a little more about how their culture worked, I realised that about 80 percent of the things the husbands did were done at the instigation of the women themselves. However, the way they talked about it made it sound as if their husbands were just doing it all out of love.

I got mixed up myself and began asking my husband why he wasn't doing this and that for me. But when I sat down and thought about those things – cooking, washing dishes, cleaning the house – I realised that it made no sense for me to wait all day long for him to come home to cook or wash the dishes. I got some help out of my dilemma from an unexpected source. In those days our landlords were older people in their seventies. The lady was a good friend of mine. I enjoyed talking to her more than to someone my own age. Chet and I often spent afternoons on their porch chatting and having tea. The 'boys' would talk about business and the economy, and we ladies would talk about cooking, about what kind of food people in different countries ate, what life was like in Canada 50 to 60 years ago, and about how things had changed since then. After we had been living with them for two years, they knew more about my home in Africa than the people I had been in school with for four years.

The life the two old people lived was the kind of life I always thought married people should have. It was like the life I saw when I was growing up in my family. Each person knew exactly what he or she would be doing the next day. There was dignity in each person's contribution to the family. And each person respected the work of his or her spouse.

I asked the woman what she thought of the women's movement. She said she didn't have much to say about it except that it seemed to her that all over the world people were getting mixed up. Some countries were having wars, others were having famines, and here women were demanding equality. The old man cut into our conversation.

'Listen to me, Jane, if you don't mind my telling you what my opinion is,' he said. 'Some people may wish to be young again to start their lives anew, but for me, I'm glad I have lived the life I've lived.'

He went on to tell me that nothing in this generation was safe. Everything was changing very quickly. Ten years ago he could still watch television and laugh, but now there was nothing but sex and violence. This was not to mention the newspaper where it was impossible to read more than two lines without the phrase 'nuclear power'. He was worried about the younger generation; the world was very dangerous for them, but they didn't seem to see it.

When I heard what the old man told me, I realised that North America was not what I had thought it was. His conversation made me realise that the whole world was really changing. It was like listening to my grandmother when she was 90 years old. When I had told her that people had gone to the moon, she said she was glad she had lived when she had because this was a very dangerous generation to be alive in. She said the only thing this generation hadn't done yet was to carry the flame of a fire on their heads, but she was sure that they would. She only wished that when they did, she wouldn't be around.

I was very lucky that I had found these two old people to talk to. Without them I would never have known that Canadian people had their own culture and history. I find that North American people have no patience for talking about the past. It has very little use – there is no money in it, it has no 'future' prospects and no potential for competition.

After a few years we bought a house of our own in a suburb of London, Ontario. Leaving the two old people was a little sad because during the four years I had been with them I felt I had found a new family in Canada. Then again, I thought it would be good to be alone so I could learn to establish myself independently. It was the first time I was at home during the day for any length of time. For the first few weeks I spent three hours every day on the phone listening to people trying to sell me things. I can still remember a few of their routines. One of them went like this:

'Hello, is this the lady of the house?'

'Yes, it is.'

'I have wonderful news for you! You have been selected to be our winner for today . . . Are you still there?'

'Yes.'

'You will be winning $500 or a microwave oven, or a set of salt and pepper shakers.'

The woman went on talking like a radio. Finally I asked her what I had done to be selected.

'Nothing, and all you have to do now is give a recommendation for our product. You don't have to buy anything at all. All we need is half an hour of your time.'

When I heard this I thought it was a good deal for $500. I didn't even remember the salt and pepper shakers.

'Sure, come over anytime,' I said.

The salesman brought a vacuum cleaner. He overstayed by a full hour and insisted on leaving the vacuum cleaner with me telling me I could make my mind up later. This was even after I had told him that I had no money. The machine sat in the house, and I didn't know what to do. Finally, a friend and I managed together to bulldoze the salesman into taking it back. After all that struggle, all I won was a salt and pepper shaker set.

After that I thought I had a sure-fire method. Any time someone called, I just told them that I already had whatever it was that they were advertising. However, one night in the middle of February the phone rang.

'Hello, this is the Forest Funeral Home,' the voice said. 'Have you arranged your funeral, Mrs Creider?'

'Can you repeat what you just said, please,' I asked.

The woman repeated herself, but I still didn't understand. She had called me at a time when my health was not very good, and in fact I had just seen an endocrinologist the previous week. The doctor had told me I had nothing to worry about but I had never heard of anyone making a house call to advertise a funeral, so I thought perhaps the doctor had known I was dying, but hadn't wanted to tell me. I asked the woman when the doctor had said that I was going to die. She explained to me that this didn't have anything to do with the doctor, but it was something that everyone had to do – to arrange their death. I was shocked; it was a good thing I had a strong heart, or I would have dropped dead on the spot.

To develop my own life and to keep from going out of my mind with such nonsense I decided to go to the university to take courses at night when my husband was at home to look after the baby. I wanted to take up clay sculpting. I had learned the craft as a child in Africa from local potters and I wanted to develop what talent I had.

At the university I met many women who were in my situation; they were tired of staying at home all day long and wanted to get out to do something and meet new people. However, they had plans and expectations of being something when they got out of the university. Everyone was going to find an occupation with a title as soon as they could. Everyone except me that is. I didn't have any expectations other than making myself happy. I had my family and I didn't think I could just set them aside. When I went to the university, that was something to do in my spare time, not the other way around.

I'm sure that the women there found me weird. When they asked me what I was going to do when I finished I said I would go on being a parent. But I could understand their need for equality. The husband went to work every day and met new people. In the evening he didn't want to talk. The poor woman who had been running around all day after the children felt she wasn't wanted. The husband on the other hand was thinking about how tired he was and wishing his wife would see that. This type of life seemed to me to be going on all over the city.

The men going to work are divided into three groups. Some like sports, and when they come home they just want to sit in front of the television and watch a game. Others like to come home and read a newspaper without being bothered. The third group is made up of scientists and professors who love their job so much that it doesn't matter where they are – they just continue to work. They will even bring their work to the dinner table. The only place they don't work is in the shower.

In addition I think men have been a bit selfish and have loved their women only the way they wanted to. They spend more time wrapped up in their jobs, and don't take time to appreciate what their wives have done at home. They don't see how nice it is to come home to a clean, warm house with the dinner ready and the children well-taken care of. Men don't notice that their wives have made a significant contribution because they haven't earned money. And then the wives begin to believe that they haven't really worked either and they become discontented. When they ask for this or that, the men don't have time to think because they are too busy; they just say yes quickly in order to get rid of them. Now things have got so bad I think sometimes there may be a war between men and women. The women are demanding more, and the men feel that they don't have any more to give. Also it seems to me that those women who have become doctors and lawyers and professors still don't value their own work unless they can get men to notice them. They think other women are poor judges of talent. Only, if other women are so second class, how can they feel good about being women? These women measure their success by how far they have come with respect to their male competitors. They seem to think that there is no value or dignity in a clean house, happy children or a balanced budget. I think that it is wrong to think that the only important things to do are the things that men do. Anyway, I have always thought that while men are stronger than women, so that in that respect we are not equal, women are much more clever than men.

If a white woman is a housewife, she does not see herself as a partner in her marriage. She thinks she is subordinate. She takes a low-paying job as a clerk in a store and pays all of her wage to a babysitter just so she can say that she is not a housewife. But, she gets home and the toilets need to be scrubbed, the children still need supper. She has two whole jobs instead of one and no extra money to show for it.

In the Nandi tribe, a young girl will be kept in a house to look after the children, and then the mother can do what she wants. The mother can pick vegetables in the garden, grind the maize for supper and prepare the meal. The children are watched by the babysitter. By evening everyone has done their part and everyone knows which part is theirs. Every part has value.

I think that it is fine for women to be doctors and lawyers, or anything else they may wish to become, but I think that this should be a matter of choice. Women who don't want to do this should still have the right to security and dignity in doing what they want to do in raising a family. And a woman who has become a doctor or lawyer or anything else should be able to stop and raise a family without losing self-respect. Our custom of women caring for children is a very old one, perhaps as old as mankind itself. Why should it be thrown out?

However, I couldn't say all that in this society because women are trapped in the middle. They think a lot about having more equality but they don't seem to want to be without men. When I thought that men were no good at all, I decided not to get married. But women here seem to need men badly.

One of the other reasons I am critical of the women's movement is that it doesn't respond to the needs of all women, from the top to the bottom of the class system. As it now stands, it only fits upper-class women who have a full-time nanny, housekeeper and cook. If you are middle class, the choice you may have to make is not to have a family at all. At least, this is what I've concluded from talking to many women. It is not that the women's movement analysis of their situation is inaccurate, it is just that the solutions they propose are not applicable to most women. Daycare centres don't solve anything. They just lead to neglected and insecure children who are treated as commodities and not given love.

People may wonder why I'm not criticising men more than I do. Many men that I've talked to have no idea what women want. Some think that women don't want to have chairs pulled out, doors opened or coats held for them because that is patronising. Others think that women want the freedom to ask men out, and that when they go out together, the woman should pay. Others think that women want equal pay for equal work. Some men think that women want them to share equally in domestic work. But the only one of the above that men care very much for is being taken out and fed by a woman. Basically there is nothing that men want from women, so they are not about to change when there is no reason for them to change.

My frustration is that women can't see that they have to get what they want by themselves rather than depending on men to do it for them. Women are not endeavouring to be independent from the system. Men may well have created the system in the first place but women shouldn't just take on the values of a society that is obsessed by power and money and try and compete within it – they should take things into their own hands and set their own standards. As it is they are manipulated by men and the system. I believe men have blinded women but women have allowed themselves to be blinded. They should just say: men can't do anything good for us; we have to do it for ourselves. So many women complain that men patronise them but I think they encourage patronage if they rely so much on what men think of them. Also if women just got on with it on their own men would be more comfortable because they wouldn't be so frightened of being devoured.

I discovered how frightened men were while working closely with young people in the art studio at university over a long period of time. The boys were extremely careful. If one of them saw that a girl had a crush on him, he would try to avoid the girl. Sometimes they would come to talk to me. They said that if you asked a girl out once, things were all right. The second time would be so-so, and by the third, things would be getting sticky. The girl would start talking about children, about what kind of mother she wanted to be, etc. The boy would begin to wonder who she was going to have those children with.

'I haven't even asked her to marry me, and she has started talking about children already,' the boy would say.

I found it very hard to answer the boys' questions. The only thing I could think was that maybe a woman doesn't know what a man wants when he asks her out, so she makes a point of talking about children to see if the relationship has any future.

When I talked with the girls, however, it was a different story. If a girl had gone out with a boy a few times, she might say, 'Oh boy, I've been seeing this guy for couple of days, and I'm beginning to like him a lot.' When I heard the differences between these two groups of young people, I was amazed. I was also shocked to see young men being afraid of girls because they didn't want responsibility. I had begun to think that men in North America had run out of luck; they wouldn't be able to control women any more. But after being with these young people, I changed my mind.

It also continues to be a mystery to me how men manage to turn everything they do into something worthwhile while women have been doing housework across the world for thousands of years, and have never been able to turn it into something special. I'm confident that if housework were men's work, they would have turned it into something important by now. I'm sure that if they had found anything interesting in it they would have taken it over already in the same way they have taken over other things that women used to do. Even something like cooking can make them famous. Women still cook, even today, but there are no great chefs who are women. If cooking was going to make anyone famous, it should certainly have made a woman famous first.

All over the world for generations, women have been midwives. As you may remember, I have known myself how to be a midwife since I was nine years old. Every time I have delivered a baby I have enjoyed the experience. Before I came to Canada, I was taught by my grandmother how to look after pregnant women. When I left my country I knew quite a bit about women – maybe half of what a gynaecologist knows.

When I had been in Canada for a while I had to look for a midwife for a check-up. My husband told me to ask our family doctor for a gynaecologist. The word 'gynaecologist' itself sounded outrageous to me. I wondered why they weren't just called 'midhusbands'. An appointment was made but as soon as I got into the changing room I was shocked. The tools (I guess they should be called instruments, but that's another unnecessary big word like the name of the medical specialty) gave the room an impressive appearance. Some of them looked like scissors, others like levers for prying, and some looked like can-openers. I said to myself, 'Mercy me, where is he going to can-open me?' I wondered if I had come to a garage instead of a doctor.

The doctor checked me over, and when he had finished he tried to explain what he had found, but I couldn't understand him. The language he spoke might as well have come from another planet. When he finished he asked me if I had any questions. I didn't know what to reply because I hadn't understood a word he said. I just asked him to tell me one thing – if the sickness I had was bad or could it be cured. I also asked him to answer me in plain English. He said he would give me some medicine, but that I should also come back in two weeks.

When I realised I wasn't going to understand what the doctor said to me, I decided to find a woman gynaecologist. I asked my family doctor and, to my complete surprise, he told me that there weren't any women doctors in that field in our town. I asked why, but all he could say was that maybe they weren't interested. Still I thought that surely in this day and age there would be a woman to protect women's privacy.

Instead I got the feeling that women no longer felt that this was their job.

My observations here come through curiosity and not exclusively from my personal experiences. I wanted to find out what the position of a married woman in North-American, English-speaking culture was. I was married to someone from this culture. So I had to talk to many English-speaking women in North America. I was also very curious to find out about the women's movement. I don't want to be around something important happening to women and not be part of it. I found out that it was an attempt to create a foundation which didn't previously exist, and that it really was only helpful for women with a good job. It didn't address the problems of women who were primarily homemakers, and, in fact, to a certain extent it seems to have removed what little dignity there previously had been in what they did. And as for those women who were working, it seemed to me that what they were primarily doing was measuring their success with respect to men instead of creating a specialness around and for themselves. I guess what I was looking for really was the sense of their importance that Nandi women have. When you are grown up, you have a place in life which is created for you by the way the society is organised and you can be sure of your own importance. You are secure and don't need to go after men to be assured that you are worth something. The place of a Nandi woman is this: when a woman is married, she acquires rights to a house and property (both land and livestock) which she manages and will pass on to her children. These aren't provided for her by her husband (in the way that they are in white society and which creates a situation where white women are dependent on their husbands unless they work), but are simply part of the way the society is organised. They belong to the woman by inalienable right, just as her children can't be taken from her (or her husband for that matter, since we have no divorce). It actually doesn't even matter if a woman has no children. She still has the same secure place and rights and is in no way dependent on her husband.

I guess what I want to say is that I was terrified by the competitiveness of North America. I had the feeling, being a woman in North America, that the society provided no security. A woman had no place unless she did exactly what a man did. Otherwise she was secure only as long as she was with a husband. And this kind of security, where you were dependent on someone, was new to me and was terrifying. It was unbelievable as well to me that nearly all the women I talked to felt totally or nearly totally insecure. I couldn't believe that a society as 'advanced' as North American society was could be so cruel as to deny half of the people in it a basic sense of worth. What good did it do to argue competitively for 'equal pay' for 'equal jobs' when most women didn't have jobs or had jobs that were themselves degrading, such as being a salesperson in a low-quality department store?

An issue which affects all this is inheritance, and I should explain how it works in Nandi. A Nandi man may marry several wives, and it is obviously important that one wife should not be able to monopolise everything a man has. This is one of the reasons why a woman is so independent of her husband with respect to her house, land and property. A man does not have any right to take something from one wife and give it to another. But this is exactly what happens all the time in North American society. If a woman dies, and her husband remarries, the first wife's children are entirely at the mercy of the second wife, since most couples have joint ownership of all of their property and when a woman dies her husband then owns it all automatically. A disaster like this actually happened to a friend of mine. His mother died, his father remarried and even though he and his new wife never had any children, when the father died, none of the property passed on to his children. The second wife kept it all for herself and her relations. In another case, the husband of a childless couple died, and his wife, instead of respecting his wishes, wrote a will giving everything to her family and nothing to his even though the estate they lived on had been in his family for almost a century and a half. When my husband and I went to have a will drawn up, and I asked to write in that such and such amounts would go to the children, the lawyer looked at me as though I was crazy. There was apparently no way for property which was held in common to be willed by one of the co-owners. This is another right that I think women in North American society should be campaigning for.

Figuring out the position of women in North American society, I realised that I couldn't keep up with the competition. I had to make a choice like the first Tapsubei did. I didn't want to live free and unattached to anything, so I made a decision which I thought would allow me to live without the feeling that I was being 'looked after' by my husband. I decided that when I went back to Africa I would buy a farm on the understanding that my husband was free to live with me there but that it would be my property since it was in Nandi and came under my people's customs.

Although I had been in North America for seven years, there were many things I still didn't understand. Something which really amazed me and which I find very hard to understand is the life of old people.

When we were growing up as Nandi children, we were always taught that older people were very important. We were also taught that they knew more than we did. If any older person asked you to do anything for her you were taught to simply do it, even if the person wasn't related to you in any way. We were also taught to let them have their way; no matter what we couldn't disagree with them. The only way you could get out of something an older person asked you to do was to persuade your parents to get you out of it.

I used to be sure that getting old was a good thing. You would have everybody paying attention to everything you said. However, since I have been in North America I'm no longer sure.

When I was growing up, if there was any fun going around, my grandmother was the first to tell me. My parents never sat down with us and told us things the way my grandmother would. My grandmother Gogo was very tall and beautiful and she had lived a successful life. Ever since she had been a child, people had admired her looks, and she had always felt that she was someone special. All of her life she kept a personal idea of what beauty was in a little place in her mind.

At night I would spend hours listening to her tell me what she was like when she was young. I felt I was watching a movie that had been made 80 years ago. Listening to her made me think my life wasn't as exciting as hers had been. I felt that I would never have anything to tell young people when I got old myself. When I sit and remember, I feel things haven't been so good for me.

Between the time I talked to my grandmother and now, I have travelled all over the world. If I hadn't made my home in North America, I would know that when I was old, I would have many things to tell young people. But in Canada I have been more frightened of being old than proud of what I have done in my life.

When I first came here, it took me a long time to find out what the lives of old people were like. The people I knew were university professors. None of them had old parents with them and they rarely mentioned parents. This seemed pretty weird to me. My parents were certainly not the best in the world, but a day could not pass without my at least mentioning them.

Since I met a lot of old people at bus stops, I knew they existed. I had no idea how they lived, however, until one day when I was looking in the newspaper classified ads for a used chest of drawers. I answered an ad and spoke to an old lady who said she had a lot for sale and I could come over and see them if I wanted, she was about 75 and was selling virtually everything in her house. I bought quite a few things from her, and after I had paid her, she asked me where I came from. I told her from Africa, and she said that I must need a lot for my home then.

'Yes, I do,' I told her, 'but I don't have money for any more.'

'Of course not; I know young people don't have a lot of money,' she said.

She got up and went to her basement. After a little bit, she came up with some clothing.

'Do you think you might have use for these?' she asked.

'Yes, I certainly would,' I told her, 'but why are you giving your clothes away?'

'If you can use them, it will make me happy to know that someone who needed them is using them,' she said. 'I'm going to move to an old people's home. I'm over 70 years old, I have arthritis, and I can't manage by myself in this house.'

I didn't understand what an 'old people's home' was. I had never heard the phrase before, and I wondered if it meant that the person who was going there was going to die. Sometimes my people call where an old person goes after death their home. If children ask where an old person is who has died they are told that the person has gone home.

The old lady showed me some of the things she was going to take with her.

'I'm going to take this and that because they are the things I don't want to part with,' she said. 'These things have been in my family for generations. Some belonged to my grandparents.'

Now I was beginning to understand that she didn't mean death. Her situation was beginning to sound like an orphan's. I thought that maybe she didn't have any children or relatives. She asked me if I would like to look through all of her clothing to see if there was anything I could use. She started pulling things out of a garbage bag: a pair of bedsheets, children's clothing, curtains, and a lot of little things. I was shocked to see the children's clothes because I had concluded she didn't have any.

That evening, when my husband arrived home, I didn't even give him a chance to sit down before I asked him what 'old people's home' was. He told me that it was a place where old people went to live when they could no longer look after themselves.

'What kind of old people go there?' I asked. 'Just the ones who don't have any children, or all old people?'

'Every old person goes. It doesn't have anything to do with having or not having children,' he said.

'How long do they stay there?' I asked.

'As long as they live,' was his answer.

I didn't want to ask any more, but decided I would find out more by myself. I went to visit an old people's home. I didn't know anyone, so I just sat down and watched three old men talking to each other. They were very nice to one another. One was older than the other two and I could also see that they showed him respect because he was older. After I had been there for about 20 minutes, one of the men asked me if I was a new worker. I said I wasn't but I had just come to visit them. We talked together for about half an hour. Then a few more old people came. Some of them were in wheelchairs. The workers seemed to talk to the old people as though they were trying to cheer them up. However, it appeared to me that they talked to them more as though they were dogs, cats or four-month-old children. I could see no good reason for putting old people in homes. My visit didn't do me any good either; it made me feel I was watching a crime being committed before my eyes. I had told myself that daily living in North America was easier. No matter how late I was in preparing a meal, it was always possible to eat food from packages called TV dinners. Not until when I visited those old people did I realise that living in North America was not all it was cracked up to be.

It is hard to understand who decided to separate old people from their families. I may have interpreted old people's homes as a sin or a crime, but this is not what old people themselves think even though they know they are not living a very good life. I don't know how old people were brainwashed into believing that they had to go to these homes in order not to appear selfish. Although the old people know that the custom is torture, they also feel that there isn't any alternative. They would like to say to the younger generation, 'If you people want to help us, help us to stay at home with our own families. Since money has to be spent anyway, why not spend it in a good way instead of keeping us in a state of day-by-day uncertainty.'

But the old people don't want to complain, because they don't want to be the ones to break the custom that has been made for them. I'm not sure whether the young people in North America know that a young person today is going to be an old person tomorrow; if they did they would have made a better life for old people because they would know they themselves would be next. I also don't know whether they realise that someone's heart never stops wanting happiness no matter how old they are. What I have written also should not be understood as meaning that North Americans are bad or that they don't care about other people. North Americans are unbelievably good and honest. They are willing to help people in other countries. After living with them for more than eight years, I can say that they are charming and easy to live with. They mind their own business and tend to be peaceful as well.

The only thing I wonder is why the people themselves don't see what I see as a problem. In trying to find an answer I can say that time means a lot to North Americans. Also they don't like to make sacrifices for things that won't make them look clever. At first when I noticed that they didn't like to waste time, I thought they wanted to work hard to make a lot of money. Now I have changed my mind. I think that what they are really after is competition. No one wants to do something for nothing; everything has to mean something, and taking care of old people is a responsibility, not a challenge for them. I even think that what is really bothering women here is that housework is not challenging.

In addition to requiring challenges constantly, I think people here also have unusually large requirements for freedom. They need the freedom, I suspect, in order to have time to challenge each other. People will go to incredible lengths to be free. They are willing to get married, but they are also equally willing to get divorced if that will make them free. The complications of lawyers, time, money, name-calling, and so on, ought to be enough to deter anyone from divorce but not when freedom is the object. And not just once, but often many times. I sometimes wonder why people don't arrange their divorces before they marry, with a contract which gives them the right to separate any time they want to. Maybe this would put the lawyers out of business. I like freedom, but I think that too much freedom is a not good thing because it makes the society too disorganised for people to be happy.

CHAPTER TWELVE
Back to Africa

I had been away from my birthplace for eight years, since I was 25 years old. I was getting old and grey! My parents were also getting old, and I even feared that I might not recognise them. Also they hadn't seen my family, my husband and our son Colin. So in 1980 I went back home to my birthplace in East Africa.

It was a long flight and very tiring but, when we arrived in Kenya in the morning and I saw my brother and other relatives and friends waiting at the airport, I was very excited. I had left Kenya eight years ago, but coming back it still seemed the same. The only thing I could see that had definitely changed were the prices. Everything was very expensive. I have never felt as poor as I felt the day we arrived. The taxi from the airport cost £10, although it was only four miles. When I left Kenya, it had only cost about £1. Being in North America I had changed in various ways, but it really hit me when I realised that I should have bargained with the taxi driver. I had completely forgotten about bargaining!

While I was away I had only thought of Africa in terms of my own people and my parents. I had forgotten about all the other tribes and people that lived there. Now I had to bring all that knowledge back into operation.

The first thing we did was look for a hotel. We thought we would be able to find a decent one for around £20 a night, but instead that was the bottom of the barrel. A decent hotel was about £40, and even then it had absolutely hopeless beds. They were too short and they sagged in the middle. When you got into the bed, the heavy part of your body would sink down three feet, and the light part would stick up in the air. To make matters worse, my husband weighs a good deal more than I do, so he would sink down three feet, and I would fall on top of him.

The first night was a disaster with a style all its own. In the morning my husband decided to get a car and look for another hotel. He went ahead and checked out and I completely forgot that I wouldn't be safe on my own with the baby. I had to pay someone to carry our suitcases to the lobby. At the bottom of the stairs was a large assortment of people, some of whom were waiting to get their hands on whatever they could. None of our suitcases had locks and they were so heavy that they had to be carried downstairs one at a time. I didn't trust the man who was carrying the luggage so I had to follow him down when he carried a suitcase downstairs, then I had to follow him back up the stairs to get another suitcase. With a child under my arm it was not easy. Finally all of the luggage was down. I thought I had managed everything successfully, but later that day when I opened the suitcases, I discovered that two of my son's sweaters were gone. Better than losing a whole suitcase I thought.

I hadn't seen my parents yet, but I was ready to leave. If Chet had said that we should turn around and go back to Canada, I would have instantly agreed. We spent a week in Nairobi, and the only time I was happy was when my brother came with his friends to go out with us. We only stayed there to buy a car, and when we couldn't find one we could afford, we went up-country to a town called Kericho to get one. We were then set to go to visit my parents. This was of course an undertaking requiring considerable thought. If I went to see my mother first, my father would say that I had gone to my mother to be ruined. If I went to see my father first, my mother would take that to mean that I loved him more than I loved her. I decided to go to the one who would be most hurt if I didn't go there first. That would be my mother. She is also hardest to deal with when she gets upset.

We got there at ten in the morning. She had been waiting for us ever since we had arrived in Kenya, so she assumed we had already been to see my father. She was very happy to see my family, but it didn't take her long to ask me how my father was. I was shocked to see that absolutely nothing had changed over the last eight years. Instead of giving me credit for living on my own, they treated it as an opportunity to get back at one another through me. It was clear that my mother was looking for a squabble since she really didn't want to know how my father was at all. I had just arrived, and here an argument was about to start! I told my mother that I hadn't seen Father for over eight years.

'Thank goodness you haven't gone to see him,' she said, 'because you have a lot to learn about him.'

'Mother, if you have to tell me about what my father has done wrong while I've been away, please don't do it now,' I said. 'I came to see you and talk to you. I have a lot to ask you about: my brothers, sisters and cousins – how many of them are married and with children?'

Mother stubbornly refused to stop talking about my father. She insisted that I had to listen, and I finally gave up.

'Your father was really upset when he heard that you had married a European,' she said. 'He had a temper tantrum and accused me of letting you disgrace the family. I tried to tell him I knew nothing about it but he wouldn't listen to me, and in the end I decided to sue him. Your father has done nothing for me except cause me endless pain.

'Suing your father was my way of discovering all of the terrible things he has been saying about me since we separated. I wanted him to pay for the damage he did to me and my child. I know the reason you ended up marrying a foreigner has to do with the way he raised you. He raised you without love. If he had let me raise you maybe things would have been different. In court when your father was called to the stand to reply to my charges, he said that they weren't true. He said that he had been separated from me for 25 years. He also said that when we got married, we had three children, two boys and one girl. The two boys didn't survive, and I kept the girl with me. He said the first he heard about you was that you had fled the country to go to North America. The next thing was that you had got married to a European, and the last thing was that he was being sued.

' "I feel like this woman is confused about who she should be suing,' your father said, "She should be suing that white man to get her daughter back instead of me."

' "Was your daughter with you when she went to North America?" the judge asked me, and when I said yes, he said, "Case dismissed."

'I thought everything was finished, but three weeks later I was sent a warrant saying I had to appear in court the next week. Your father had learned there is a thing called "divorce" that he wanted to use on me. I went to court and your father divorced me. When I asked what about our daughter, he told me that I had custody of you.'

I knew Mother wouldn't make things up but I also knew that Father would never say anything bad about me. I realised that what he had said in the court was probably to save his neck. I think that my father was probably more disappointed than anything else; he couldn't believe that his daughter had flown the country and married a white man. Marrying anyone from another society with my people is like poisoning the name of the family. It shows that you have no class, that you are mentally ill, and that you are no use at all. Marrying a white man especially means that you are only after money, and that there is no love involved at all. That bothered my father a lot because he thought that no child of his should need money.

Although I had just heard that things were sour between my father and me, I still intended to see him because we were as much close friends as father and daughter. We both think the same way, and even today when he is in his late fifties, his thoughts don't sound out-dated to me. He must have thought my mother had had something to do with my marrying a person from another society because I was too much like him in character to do it on my own.

When we left, my mother asked me if I still intended to visit my father. I told her I definitely was. All my life I have been hiding my vists to one from the other. When I went to see my mother, I would tell my father I was visiting a friend, and when I went to see my father I would tell my mother the same thing. This time I decided to tell the truth to both of them if they asked me. I had to recognise that they would never change. I had lied for many years to avoid hurting them, but it didn't appear to have helped a bit.

Father was so happy to see us that he didn't even seem to notice that my husband was not Nandi. He didn't mention going to court with my mother, and I didn't ask. I felt that if he wanted to tell me, he could do it by himself.

We spent the day with my stepmothers, and my young brothers and sisters. All my other sisters had been married. Only one my age was at home visiting. She and I cooked together and my father and Chet were talking. I heard my father ask him if we had been to my mother's yet.

'Yes we have,' my husband said.

'How was she?' father asked. 'Did she say anything at all to your wife?'

'They were talking in Nandi, and I couldn't understand,' my husband said.

My father is like me. He doesn't know how to get someone to tell him something. He gives up right away when he doesn't get the answer he is hoping to hear.

Throughout the time I was there, I could see he was struggling to ask me without hurting me if I was happy with the life I had chosen. I knew he wanted very much to know about me and my husband. He had no idea that two people from different cultures could marry and live a normal life. He felt pity in his heart that such a thing had to happen at all. My family knew nothing about white society, and I was not about to teach them. I struggled to live in their style. When my father gets up in the morning, breakfast is ready for him. He eats and then out he goes. My stepmother worries about the affairs of the household, and when my father comes back at noon, lunch is ready for him to eat. Out he goes again. I tried to live in that style just to convince my father that marrying a man from another society was not different from marrying a Nandi man. I also didn't want my young sisters to think that marrying a non-Nandi was something very different. I knew that if they were even to see my husband hand me a cup of tea, they would jump to all sorts of conclusions about how good such a marriage was without knowing about the problems. However, although I tried to live like a Nandi wife, that didn't seem to impress my father; it probably never occurred to him that there was any other way to do things. Father still worried about me, and several times he tried to talk to me.

'Tapsubei, you know you can choose to live the life you want,' he said. 'I have a big farm, houses and cattle. The door is open for you and your husband if you ever want to be in Africa.'

I realised father was worrying about me because he wasn't sure if I was happy with my life. One day we were sitting alone together on top of the hill beside our house. Father was telling me about what had happened during the time I had been away. All of sudden he became silent as though he were stopping to take a deep breath. I waited.

'Tapsubei, you know we haven't talked seriously,' he said. 'The only thing I know about white people is the struggle with the British. From that I certainly wouldn't describe them as good human beings. I would say that they are great warriors, but I wouldn't trust them for a moment. I have seen your husband, and like him, but how far should he be trusted? I think you should tell me about the two of you. How did his parents react when he married you?'

I found it hard to answer because my father was from an extended family and he was asking about nuclear families. In an extended family, when a person wants to do something, he goes around seeking the approval of all of his relatives. In a nuclear family everyone does what they want with their lives.

It was a good question because, although I had met my in-laws, I had never stopped to wonder what they thought of my marrying their son. This was because I already knew how a nuclear family worked. I also didn't expect them to love me. When two people from different societies marry, they only hope that no one in their family will be hurt by what they are doing. To be loved is the last thing on their minds. The couple has to sacrifice a lot for their own feelings, and when they get married, they are pretty much on their own. They are ready to give love to their families themselves, but if the families reject this love, they accept it because they knew that might happen.

I didn't tell my father that the parents in a nuclear family always respect the right of their children to do what they want. I didn't want him to think I had got married just because it was what I alone had wanted to do. I would rather have him just think I was peculiar. Since, in fact, I had no idea what my in-laws felt about me, I decided to tell him honestly that I didn't know what they thought of my marrying their son, but I imagined they probably felt much the same way he did.

'I don't think that they hate me, but that doesn't mean that if there were a contest between an ugly white girl and me that they would choose me for their son's wife! However, that also doesn't mean that they don't like me. Just like you, they didn't have any choice.'

During our discussion I told my father a little bit about marriage in Western culture in the hope that he would stop worrying. I tried to explain that people weren't glued so tightly together and if things ever got bad, they just separated. I also told my father that he could rest assured that marrying a white man was nothing like fighting a British farmer for a piece of land.

Our trip to Africa was proving to be a wonderful research opportunity for my husband. He wanted to study each of the dozen or so dialects of the Nandi language group. If any time was left, he planned to write a book as well. Being with my family gave him a lot of free time, and I had to remind him not to get too used to that style of life because it wasn't possible in North America. Everyone in Africa is changing to a more modern way of life except my family. That of course is due to my father who says that anyone who wants to change from traditional ways is mentally ill. So in my family if a man says that he is working he shouldn't be interrupted. Even when we were outside sitting with my sisters and stepmother and Chet went into the house with a book, my stepmother would say, 'Tapsubei, I think you and your sister should both talk quietly.'

'Why, Mother?' I asked.

'Because "Father Colin" has gone in to read.'

(A Nandi mother-in-law cannot refer to her son-in-law by his first or last name and so must use the name of his child to refer to him.)

'He carries a book like that everywhere he goes, mother,' I told her.

'It doesn't matter, he may decide he wants to work.'

What she said hit me with a shock. I couldn't imagine being asked to speak quietly until my husband had made up his mind whether he wanted to read or not. I told my stepmother that if I were to stop talking every time I saw him with a book, I would stop talking for ever.

My husband liked the life-style. I realised it one day when he let my father call me to change the baby. The child was standing in front of them sopping wet, and I was nowhere near. If there was anything we had shared equally it was taking care of our son. I was angry, and as I brought a diaper, I decided to say something even though my father was there. I just told Chet that God would get him for this. Father asked me what I had said, and I replied nothing, but I was frightened because I thought he had understood me.

In the last few months before we left Africa, as planned, we bought a small piece of land to farm. It was in a place I had always dreamed of living in about 100 miles from my parents. We discovered that the nearby town was a delightful place. It had been founded by the British and boasted a lovely club with all sorts of sporting facilities and a nice cosy fireplace for cold, rainy days. I had very little time for the club because I had to find people to look after the land and get the first crop planted and fertilised.

We went to Nairobi and made our travel plans. Although there were many places we wanted to see, we decided to go to Spain on our way back.

We stayed in a pleasant hotel in Madrid in a quiet residential part of the city. It was sheer luxury to us after a year of relative privation. It was especially nice to have an indoor toilet. In Africa the bath and toilet were some distance from the house and it was not until a week after we had moved in that we discovered that we were sharing these outdoor facilities with a group of other people who sneaked in there at night. We also shared the outhouses with several hundred flies and an assortment of depressed-looking spiders. Outside were a number of very anaemic dogs that contributed to the general look of squalor. Altogether the effect had made me ready to call anything with an interior bath luxurious.

I didn't speak Spanish at all, and my husband had to be my translator while we were there. The only words I learned to say were *muchas gracias* for thank you. In the evening when we went to dine, I had to watch my husband talking to the waiter, and I kept hearing those two words over and over again. It was pretty obvious what they meant because everytime the waiter brought something, my husband uttered them. Since there was nothing else to do, I started to count the number of times he said the words, and I soon reached ten. At that point I cracked up laughing. Spain was the only country where one said thank you ten times per meal! My husband didn't appreciate the joke. It was even funnier when he told me that the waiter wasn't Spanish, but Portuguese, and didn't even speak Spanish very well. I thought that maybe 'thank you' was the way to communicate with him.

We had a wonderful time in Spain visiting museums, shopping, eating beautifully prepared food, listening to Spanish music and just enjoying ourselves. We got so accustomed to the place that we could have stayed for ever, but finally we realised that we weren't home yet.

When we got back to Canada I was pleased to be there but I found myself thinking about a lot of things. I was having trouble understanding the difference between primitive and civilised. On a certain occasion I used the word primitive to describe myself and I thought that it meant simple-minded. I believed that after I came to the civilised world I would become very clever, but now I'm more confused than when I left the jungles of Africa. The word 'civilisation' no longer impresses me, and it is beginning to appear to me just like a jungle without the trees. I find that in the civilised world people can't stop and look back. They are always going forward, but they seem to be messing things up along the way. Perhaps if they could stop and clean up the messes they have made they wouldn't be as tense as they are now.

People in the civilised world think that winning is the most important thing in life. They can't even stand to lose a lousy little ball game that is supposed to be played for pleasure. They don't seem satisfied with what they have; they need more and more. People seem to care more about themselves and the jobs they do than anything else.

The people who are really in the biggest dilemma are married women. They want everything – children, a job, and freedom – but the result is not satisfactory. Women end up feeling guilty for just being wives and mothers without any job or title. People start forgetting that being a mother and a wife *is* a full-time job. Even at social gatherings it is hard to talk to people because all they want to talk about is their jobs; no one seems to want to talk about their families. That makes me understand why everyone wants a job – to have something to talk about! I find it astonishing to meet someone for the first time and to start telling them what I do. This way of putting jobs foremost also makes young married women feel insecure. How should I act when people tell me what they do? Am I supposed to look impressed?

My husband and I once went to a party where everybody was introduced by their title – doctor, professor and so on, and the hostess kept introducing me as a clay sculptor. Things had gone well for me in that department – I had a craft studio at the university, I sold sculptures at local galleries and I had been invited to teach pottery – but I didn't want to talk about it all the time. I insisted on just using my name. People kept asking me what I did. The questions were friendly enough but I had been hearing about jobs all night long and was sick of it. Finally, just to tell people something impressive, I said that I was a brain surgeon. Soon everyone in the room was laughing because some of them knew who I was and that I was just making a joke. To me it was not only a joke, but it was a way of saying that knowing what I did in my life was not important.

Occasionally I see people trying hard to find out how to be good parents. They even take courses which is also very difficult for me to understand. I would think that to be good at anything at all, you have to like it first. I also think that if people would just talk about families instead of jobs, they would learn something without having to pay money for it. As you have been raised by your parents, there are probably some good things they taught you. I can't see how anyone would want to throw away their own good-quality education in exchange for one of uncertain quality.

People sometimes ask me about racism in Canada. Maybe I am naive, but I haven't experienced discrimination here. I know it exists, but have never noticed it myself. I know who I am, an African and a Nandi, and I have never tried and never want to be anything but that. If there is anything that has helped me not to experience discrimination, it may be that I always introduce myself to neighbours as an individual, and they quickly learn that I am not a bad person. Also I have always been self-employed, so I have never had to experience discrimination on the job market. I do, however, have a strong accent, and I have noticed many times that people draw away when they don't understand me rather than try. I understand that that is because of the accent. London Ontario is a very conservative town, and people aren't used to many new sounds. Sometimes I see people being a little afraid to understand me. Other times I see in their eyes that they are confusing having an accent with not being knowledgeable, so they don't try to have an interesting conversation with me. I usually talk back to them as though they were babies when they do this. It may also help that in Nandi society, we are taught from an early age that nothing anyone who is not Nandi says or does counts for anything. Nandi don't discriminate against each other, and don't really pay much attention to what non-Nandi think or say about them.

One curious thing that surprised me very much was that in the small black community here, mostly West Indians, the lighter you are and the wavier your hair is, the better-looking you are. When you are a dark as I am, no one has any comment for you. When I introduce myself to one of these people, and say I am from Africa, they say, 'Oh, I should have known, because you are so dark.' Coming from Africa for them means darkness.

Something else which people often ask me is what it is like to be married to someone who is not from my tribe. I say it is so good that everyone should try it. What I have really learned from marrying someone different from me is to give everyone around me equal value. I have become colour-blind, and when I meet someone I don't seem to see their colour, but rather look for their personality. I have been able to make close friends with people from all tribes. Before I married I didn't even bother to understand if people from other tribes had feelings like me or to see if I could make sense of them. Today I can say to anyone that if you take time to know people you can make your home anywhere in the world. Also, although I have become colour-blind, I haven't tried to be someone other than I am.

Manny Shirazi
Javady Alley

This haunting first novel is set in Iran in the turbulent year of 1953, when working class activists are struggling to wrest the country's oil from the control of foreigners.

But we see events through seven-year-old Homa's eyes. Her world is the intensely private one of childhood, bounded by house, courtyard, and the lives of her mother and grandmother. Her ventures outside are to the women-only baths, a religious pilgrimage, or once, daringly, with neighbourhood children to the railway track.

It is only slowly that the violence of outside events begins to threaten . . .

Full of the sights, smells and sounds of daily life, Manny Shirazi's prose is at once sensuous, and direct.

Manny Shirazi grew up in Iran, and has spent much of her adult life in London, where she now lives. The Women's Press is proud to publish this outstanding new author.

Fiction   £3.95   0 7043 3928 5

Tony Cade Bambara
The Salt Eaters

Velma Henry finds herself in the Southwestern Community Infirmary facing Minnie Ransom, fabled healer and vehicle of the spirit world, when, falling on hard times, she tries to commit suicide. In facing the responsibilities of health so that she can become whole she delves, with the salt eaters – the black community – into the shared dreams of their past to find a shared vision of the future.

'A book full of marvels' *The New Yorker*

'Swirling, whirling and compelling' *Guardian*

'Toni Cade Bambara's magicians are women. Their words will bathe you in illuminations, and spread balm on bruised spirits' *Morning Star*

Fiction   £3.50   0 7043 3882 3

Alice Walker
The Color Purple
1983 Pulitzer Prize Winner
Now filmed by Steven Spielberg

'Dear God: I am fourteen years old. I have always been a good girl. Maybe you can give me a sign letting me know what is happening to me . . .' So begins Alice Walker's touching, complex and engrossing new novel about two sisters in the Deep South between the wars. Celie, raped by the man she calls her father, her two children taken from her, her sister run away, has no one to talk to but God. Until, forced into an ugly marriage, she meets Shug Avery, the singer, the magic woman; and discovers not the pain of rivalry but the love and support of women.

'A striking and consummately well written novel . . . without doubt her most impressive' *New York Times Book Review*

Fiction   £3.95   0 7043 3905 6

Alice Walker
In Search of Our Mothers' Gardens
Womanist Prose

'Womanist is to feminist as purple is to lavender'

This is a phrase from Alice Walker's own definition of the special quality of her 'womanist' prose. The depth of thought it implies is reflected throughout this major collection of the essays, reviews and articles she has written over the last fifteen years.

| Non-fiction | Paperback | £4.95 | 0 7043 3931 5 |
| | Hardcover | £12.95 | 0 7043 2845 3 |

Sharan-Jeet Shan
In My Own Name
An Autobiography

From childhood, Sharan-Jeet had a mind of her own. She chafed against the restrictions of her status as a girl in the Punjab, subject to the authority now of her father, in the future of a husband. So she set out to train as a doctor, but when she fell in love with a Muslim the full wrath of her Sikh family descended upon her. She was taken out of medical school, locked up, beaten, and eventually forced into an arranged marriage . . .

Even when her marriage carried her to a strange country, she didn't give up. The story of how she struggled to assert her own autonomy and establish a home of her own is one of extraordinary courage, faith and determination.

Black and Third World Women's Studies
Autobiography   Paperback   £3.95   0 7043 3974 9

Ellen Kuzwayo
Call Me Woman

Ellen Kuzwayo now lives in Soweto, the sprawling black township outside Johannesburg. But she grew up in the 1920s and 30s on her family's beautiful farm near Thaba 'Nchu in the Orange Free State. That land was forcibly 'purchased' by the South African Government in the 1970s, as part of its policy of removing so-called 'black spots' from areas allocated to whites.

The author writes about the women in her family, the girls she taught as a young woman, her colleagues in social and political life, and the women who shared political imprisonment with her in the 1970s.

Call Me Woman is a classic of rediscovered women's history.

Autobiography/Politics   Paperback   £4.95   0 7043 3936 6
                                                 Hardcover   £9.95   0 7043 2848 8